HANDS ON: THE ART OF CRAFTING IN IRELAND

HANDS ON

The Art of Crafting in Ireland

Sylvia Thompson

LIBERTIES

First published in 2012 by
Liberties Press
7 Rathfarnham Road | Terenure | Dublin 6W
T: +353 (1) 405 5701
www.libertiespress.com | info@libertiespress.com

Trade enquiries to Gill & Macmillan Distribution
Hume Avenue | Park West | Dublin 12
T: +353 (1) 500 9534 | F: +353 (1) 500 9595 | E: sales@gillmacmillan.ie

Distributed in the UK by
Turnaround Publisher Services
Unit 3 | Olympia Trading Estate | Coburg Road | London N22 6TZ
T: +44 (0) 20 8829 3000 | E: orders@turnaround-uk.com

Distributed in the US by
Dufour Editions | PO Box 7 | Chester Springs | Pennsylvania 19425

ISBN: 978-1-907593-43-7
2 4 6 8 10 9 7 5 3 1
A CIP record for this title is available from the British Library.

Design by Fidelma Slattery @ Someday
Printed in Poland by BZ Graf

CONTENTS

ACKNOWLEDGEMENTS

I would like to thank Conor Goodman, Features Editor of the *Irish Times* without whom this book would not exist. He commissioned the series, 'Hands On – Traditional Skills and Where to Learn Them', on which this book is based. I would also like to thank Liam Stebbing, *Irish Times* Weekend Review production editor for helping me source all the photographs used in the original series, some of which have been re-used in the book.

I would like to thank all the staff of Liberties Press, who have been a pleasure to work with. Right from the first meeting with publicity assistant, Alice Dawson and publisher, Sean O'Keeffe to working with Clara Phelan at the proofing stages and planning the launch with Caroline and Alice, it has been an enjoyable experience. Special thanks to designer, Fidelma Slattery whose personal flair has enhanced the book greatly. It's great to see that the attention to detail required for quality book publishing is still valued.

I would also like to sincerely thank all the craftspeople who were happy that material used in the *Irish Times* series be re-published for this book. Through meetings, phone conversations and emails, they transmitted their personal dedication and passion for what they do – in spite of the economic challenges that this sometimes poses. Many of them also shared their knowledge of the history of each craft for this book.

Finally, I would like to thank my family – my husband, Des Fox, an artist and our daughters, Kaitlin, Beulah and Juliette – whose everyday creativity inspires me to share that of others featured in this book.

THE ART OF MAKING

Jeanette Winterson

The most satisfying thing a human being can do – and the sexiest – is to make something. Life is about relationships – to each other – and to the material world. Making something is a relationship. The verb is the clue. We make love, we make babies, we make dinner, we make sense, we make a difference, we make it up, we make it new . . . True, we sometimes make a mess but creativity never was a factory finish.

The wrestle with material isn't about subduing; it is about making a third thing that didn't exist before. The raw material was there, and you were there, but the relationship that happens between maker and material allows the finished piece to be what it is. And that allows a further relationship to develop between the piece and the viewer or the buyer.

Both relationships are in every way different from mass production or store-bought objects that, however useful, are dead on arrival. Anyone who makes something finds its life, whether it's Michelangelo releasing David from 20 tons of Carrara marble, or potter Jane Cox spinning me a plate using the power of her shoulders, the sureness of her hands, the concentration of her mind.

I have a set of silverware made by an eighteenth-century silverworker called Hester Bateman, one of the very few women working in flatware at that time. When I eat with her spoons, I feel the work and the satisfaction that went into making them – the handle and bowl are in equal balance – and I feel a part of time as it really is, not chopped into little bits, but continuous. She made this beautiful thing, it's still here, and I am here too, writing my books, eating my soup, two women making things across time.

I feel connection, respect, delight. And it is just a spoon . . . But the thing about craft, about the making of everyday objects that we can have around us, about the making of objects that are beautiful and/or useful, is that our everyday life is enriched.

How is it enriched? To make something is to be both conscious and concentrated – it is a fully alert state, but not one of anxious hyper-arousal. We all know the flow we feel when we are absorbed in what we do.

I find that by having a few things around me that have been made by someone's hand and eye and imagination working together, I am prevented from passing through my daily life in a kind of blur.

I have to notice what is in front of me – the table, the vase, the hand-blocked curtains, the thumb prints in the sculpture, the lettering block. I have some lamps made by Marianna Kennedy, and what I switch on is not a bulb on a stem; it is her sense of light. So I am in relationship to the object and in relationship to the maker. This allows me to escape from the anonymity and clutter of the way we live now. Instead of surrounding myself with lots of things I hardly notice, I have a few things that also seem to notice me. No doubt this is a fantasy, but . . . The life of objects is a strange one.

A maker creates something like a fossil record. She or he is imprinted in the piece. We know that energy is never lost, only that it changes its form, and it seems to me that the maker shape-shifts her/himself into the object. That is why it remains a living thing.

Of course it is possible to design an object that will be made by others, but that is an extension of the creative relationship, not its antithesis. It is the ceaseless reproduction of meaningless objects that kills creativity for all of us, as producers and consumers. But are producers and consumers who we want to be?

To make is to do. It is an active verb. Creativity is present in every child ever born. Kids love making things.

There are different doses and dilutions of creativity, and the force is much stronger in some than in others – but it is there for all of us, and should never have been separated off from life into art.

I would like to live in a creative continuum that runs from the child's drawing on the fridge to Lucien Freud, from the coffee cups made by a young ceramicist to Grayson Perry's pots.

We don't need to agonise over the boundaries between 'art' and 'craft', any more than we should be separating art and life. The boundary is between the creative exuberance of being human, and the monotony of an existence dependent on mass production – objects, food, values, aspirations.

MAKING IS PERSONAL.
MAKING IS SHARED.
MAKING IS A CELEBRATION OF WHO WE ARE.

A HISTORY OF CRAFT IN IRELAND

The Crafts Council of Ireland

Craftsmanship has been a part of Irish culture since the dawn of time. Over the centuries the objects made in Ireland have changed, but craft's cultural and economic contribution has been consistent and strong. Craftsmanship, both ancient and modern, is part of our national identity and often the flagship for how Ireland is seen abroad. Historic craft spans a multitude – from the splendid metalwork of the Golden Age to the simple baskets that played a part in daily life up to a few generations ago – and its value ranges from our finest and to our most humble objects.

Our ancient history is understood through craftsmanship. The fine stone-carving of the passage graves at Newgrange is testimony to the skill of our earliest workers in stone while the torcs and lunulae of the Bronze Age, made in engraved and beaten gold, are more sophisticated than any made elsewhere. From these early beginnings, craft unfolded. With the coming of Christianity in the 5th century, decorative patterns in metal and stone evolved into human and animal forms. High crosses across the country told stories of religious escapades in stone and the fantastical illustration of the Books of Durrow and Kells established Ireland's reputation for the finest illuminated manuscripts. In the same era, the metal-working tradition, now including enamelling and gold filigree, achieved its Golden Age. These were the days of the Ardagh Chalice, the Tara Brooch, and other treasures now in the National Museum of Ireland. During this time Irish craft developed a relationship with colour and intricate patterning that has been echoed throughout the centuries. Irish craft did not evolve in isolation and influences from Britain and beyond often shaped the way that things were made. The Middle Ages saw great changes in church building which, although part of a European reform movement, acquired a distinctively Irish accent in their carved stone decoration. The Normans gave us our great Gothic cathedrals and splendid castles, and some of the finest medieval craftwork is church-based.

The colonial disruptions of the seventeenth century did not favour the making or the preservation of craft but the relative calm of the eighteenth century brought us the decorative plasterwork and pretty fanlights of our Georgian houses as well as vibrant creative industries in silver, glass, and furniture. These, although initially following British fashions, soon evolved an Irish flourish. Silverware reached its heights in the mid-eighteenth century and this too was the heyday of Irish glassware. Waterford glass, notable for its distinctive deep diamond cutting, was coveted across several continents. Irish Georgian furniture was often made for export – immense sideboards with clawed and hairy feet were more popular in America than in Ireland!
Few ordinary Irish people could afford silver, or glass, or mahogany furniture, but craftsmanship extended across all levels of society. Irish country furniture, simply and locally made, has its own

vernacular tradition and many country crafts were made by farming and fishing folk for their own use. Cloth was spun and woven in people's own homes and boats and baskets made by those who needed them. Other crafts, like coopering, were handed down within families for generations and the blacksmith's forge at the crossroads had a special place in Irish country life.

In the nineteenth century, craft was also used to generate employment by both private philanthropists and state-sponsored agencies who set up famine relief schemes in spinning, weaving, knitting, crochet, and lace-making. Craft also became popular as a means of artistic expression and the Celtic Revival reshaped the forms of ancient Irish craftsmanship to fit Ireland's emerging national identity. Following the upheavals of the early twentieth century, craft found a new phase of reinvention in the Kilkenny Design Workshops which, by linking art with industry, brought Irish craftsmanship into the world of international design. The ongoing special relationship between Irish craft and design innovation is the legacy of the Workshops. By 1971 Irish craft was strong and vibrant enough to need its own supporting organisation and, from this need, the Crafts Council of Ireland was born. Since then it has fostered all elements of craft and craftsmanship within its broad remit.

The current blossoming of contemporary craftsmanship is both new and old. Twenty-first-century Irish craft is innovative and explorative in form but belongs to a lineage of making that is as old as human endeavour. Professional makers adopt ancient skills to make contemporary objects, but also use new technology to reinvent traditional forms. Always important in human terms, craft is a vital expression of personal identity in an increasingly electronic world. The Year of Craft 2011 highlighted the popular resurgence of interest in making things by hand. At a time when history is throwing many of our material values into question, craft connects us with values that remain constant in times of change.

INTRODUCTION

Sylvia Thompson

When the *Irish Times* asked me to write a weekly column on traditional skills and where to learn them in celebration of the Year of Craft, I didn't realise that the series would become so popular that it would result in the commissioning of this book.

Each week, I researched a craft which would be published on the Heritage and Habitat page of the Weekend Review in the *Irish Times*. Starting with outdoor skills such as dry stone walling and hedge-laying, the column moved on to studio-based crafts such as pottery and glass, then delved into conservation skills before turning attention to stitching crafts and other home-based traditional skills.

For the book, it became necessary to extend the weekly columns beyond explaining the basics of how to master each skill and where beginners could go to learn them. We felt readers would be interested in the historical background to each craft and where they could go to see contemporary and historic pieces in museums, galleries, craft exhibitions as well as in the workshops and studios of craftspeople throughout Ireland.

Meeting and talking to these people for this book, I was struck by their diligence and perseverance in pursuing handmade creative work in far flung studios scattered throughout the country – right through a boom which brought cheap reproductions of almost everything to our shops.

Being a craftperson requires a certain stoic resistance to mass market trends as these individuals are often to the forefront of new trends – sometimes unbeknownst to themselves at the time. Equally impressive was a dedication to keeping old skills alive or reviving them. And the absolute passion in developing a piece beyond its function into an *objet d'art* – to be enjoyed purely for its aesthetics of colour, texture and form.

While researching the origins of each craft for this book, I became fascinated by the sweep of history that many skills embraced. To consider the origins of stone carving, metal smithing or even paper making, one must ponder the rise and fall of civilizations and sometimes even religious conflicts which either promoted a craft (calligraphy, for example) or held up its development (paper making, for example).

In this technological age where we take complexity for granted, it is intriguing to consider how the human imagination of former times worked out how to weave threads into intricate patterns on rugs and garments or to melt and solder various metals into delicately designed teapots that last for centuries.

Some makers/designers say that those who come on weekend workshops and summer courses are often very technologically-minded individuals who get great pleasure from making something for themselves.

It is this tactile quality of work that attracts most craftspeople to do what they do. And, it is this tactile quality of work that is important to celebrate in these times when almost everyone interacts with technology in a myriad of ways every day.

The late Justin Keating, a former chairman of the Crafts Council of Ireland put it beautifully in his introduction to the wonderful book, *Traditional Crafts of Ireland* by David Shaw-Smith. He wrote 'We need the wood and clay and stone and natural fibres speaking directly to us as part of our search to re-establish contact with nature.'

One is also tempted to say that the revival of interest in learning craft is a kind of reaction to over-consumption. Now, when we have less money, we are drawn towards making things for ourselves rather than constantly buying things. Even a music festival such as the Electric Picnic in County Laois has a green crafts zone where people can make things under the shelter of living willow sculptures. And, children are again being taught traditional crafts such as knitting in schools across Ireland.

The fulfilment gained from making something yourself – whether it's homemade jam or chutney, a candle, a bowl, a hat or a patchwork quilt – is a personal experience unique to each individual maker. I hope you find a craft or traditional skill in this book that will inspire you to go out and make something for yourself that will bring pleasure and satisfaction to you and those close to you.

STUDIO-BASED CRAFTS

POTTERY

What is it?

Pottery is the art of making something out of clay. There are hundreds of types of clay and many different approaches used to create the initial shape. There are also different styles and techniques used to decorate the piece, before firing and glazing and firing it again. The key skill required, as with many traditional crafts, is perseverance.

Pottery is one of the oldest crafts, and people have moulded and dried certain types of mud into shapes for use since the earliest times. Later, they realised that by firing the hardened clay shape, it would hold liquid. For 30,000 years, these skills were used to make pots and water pipes in traditional societies.

The Chinese developed clay objects and glazes about 3,000 years ago, learning to fire at high temperatures some time after that. The Egyptians are credited with making the first potter's wheels about 5,000 years ago. Marco Polo brought Oriental porcelains to Europe in the thirteenth century and later the Dutch, the English and the Italians developed various forms of functional ceramic objects.

The process was industrialised during the Industrial Revolution, but in the 1860s William Morris began to re-establish the workshop and guilds that were prominent during Renaissance times. In 1925, a large German workshop, the Bauhaus, inspired new trends that placed great emphasis on ceramic art and after World War II, various countries began to establish their own styles. Ceramic designs from Sweden and Japan, together with folk traditions in Mexico, Morocco, Turkey, Central and South America continue to influence individual potters working in studios throughout Europe and the United States.

What do the experts say?

The two main approaches to making pottery are throwing and hand-building. Potters who give classes will often specialise in either wheel-based work or hand-building using slabs or coils of clay or moulds. According to Marcus O'Mahony, who gives beginners pottery workshops in his pottery studio near Lismore, County Waterford (www.marcusomahony.com), 'The challenge of throwing is to get balance and control of the lump of clay using water as a lubricant on the spinning wheel'. Some people pick it up quickly and most people will be able to make a simple bowl after a day or two. Learning how to grip and centre the clay on the potter's wheel is the key. Then the clay is lifted and opened up to create the required shape. 'You've got to respond to the clay and develop an intuitive and sensitive feel for it.'

Hand-building is working directly with a soft piece of clay. The object is built up in layers, using an initial drawing, photo or paper template as a guide. 'You begin with a malleable piece of clay, form your shape, let it dry out and then trim and shave it down. The form comes alive then,' says Dublin-based ceramic artist, Michelle Maher, who gives regular classes and workshops in hand-building. Once dried, the piece is decorated. There are many different techniques used in this process, such as carving, sponging, stencilling, and adding coloured decorating slips of liquid clay. The piece is then allowed to dry further before being fired. Next comes the glazing, which according to Maher is the most difficult stage of all.

'Basically, you are applying a thin layer of glass to your piece. You can do that by pouring it on, splashing it on or dipping it into a bucket of glaze,' she says. Then, the piece has to be fired again.

How long does it take?

This can depend on a number of factors, such as how your piece evolves initially, how much decoration you put on it, how long it is left to dry out and how long it has to be fired for. The timing will be further affected by how your glazing works out and how long it has to be fired for again. Making and decorating the initial shape can take minutes or hours; Drying out can take weeks. Firing can take up to thirty-six hours, glazing takes a matter of minutes and the final firing will take another thirty hours or so.

Where can I see examples of pottery?

Pottery is one of the most commercial of all handmade crafts and the work of Irish potters is for sale in craft gift shops throughout the country. Potters also display and sell their work at craft fairs – the best of which takes place every December in the RDS, Ballsbridge, Dublin 2. The international trade fair, Showcase held in the same venue at the end of January each year, also includes a good range of contemporary pottery. The Kilkenny Design Centre in Kilkenny city and on Nassau Street, Dublin also

sells a good range of contemporary Irish pottery. Some potters also sell from their studios and demonstrate the process. For example, Louis Mulcahy's workshop in Clogher, Ballyferriter, Dingle, County Kerry has an open room in which it offers visitors a pottery experience on a drop-in basis during the summer months (www.louismulcahy.com).

Historic examples of pottery and ceramics can be seen in the National Museum of Ireland – Archaeology, Kildare Street, Dublin 2. The National Museum of Ireland – Decorative Arts, Collins Barracks, Benburb Street, Dublin 7 has an extensive collection of pottery and porcelain made in Ireland, France, Germany and Britain from the seventeenth century to the present day. The museum also houses a collection of Asian pottery from the fourteenth to the nineteenth century. The collection held at the National Museum of Ireland – Country Life, Turlough Park, Castlebar, County Mayo represents pottery used in homes throughout rural Ireland over the past 150 years. The Hunt Museum, Rutland Street, The Milk Market, Limerick City also has a significant international collection of pottery (Tel:061 312833, www.huntmuseum.com).

SIGN UP

Ceramics Ireland has a list of potters who give pottery workshops and classes on its website, www.ceramicsireland.org. Pottery classes are also available in community colleges (www.nightcourses.com), and as part of art and design courses in third level colleges throughout the country. The two-year course in crafts at Grennan Mill Craft School in Thomastown, County Kilkenny is one example (Tel:056 7724557, www.grennanmill.net).

BUY MATERIALS

There are four main suppliers: RPM Pottery Supplies, Ballymount, Dublin (Tel:01 4564277, www.rpmsupplies.com); Ulster Ceramics, Derry (Tel:44 (0)28 7941550, www.ulsterceramicspotterysupplies.com); Scarva Pottery Supplies, Banbridge, County Down (Tel:44 (0)28 40669699, www.scarva.com); and DBI, Blackrock Road, Cork City (Tel:021 4292888).

WORKING WITH LEATHER

What is it?

Traditionally, leatherworkers made functional and durable pieces, such as bags, shoes and belts that would last a lifetime, there was an abundance of Irish tanneries where leatherworkers could source their leather. Nowadays, the craft of leatherwork has, like many other textile crafts, become strongly influenced by changing fashions. Those working with leather will spend most of their time making decorative bags, belts and other clothing accessories that change from season to season. Leather is also used for restaurant and hotel menu folders and occasional pieces of furniture. The leather used is imported.

From the earliest times, the skins of animals have been used for clothing and shelter. Primitive societies in Europe, Asia and North America all developed the techniques of turning skins into leather goods independently of each other. Leather was used for clothing, footwear, belts, containers for liquids, boats and even armour. Indeed, the principle protective armour of the Roman soldier was a heavy leather shirt.

The art of tanning leather using the bark of trees (vegetable tanning) probably originated among the Hebrews. In Europe, tanners and leatherworkers united in trade guilds in the Middle Ages, as did craft workers in other fields. In the nineteenth century, vegetable tanning was supplemented by chrome tanning. This process now accounts for 80-90 percent of all tanning done today. Ireland had a long tradition of tanning leather, with tanneries scattered throughout the country until the middle of the last century.

What do the experts say?

The most important step in the process is selecting the appropriate piece of leather to work with, according to Conor Holden of Holden Leather Company in County Kerry. 'We buy our leather in the trade fairs in Bologna in Italy in June/July and

GARVAN DE BRUIR

CONOR HOLDEN

come up with designs for the following season that best suit the leather we buy. . . . Because leather is a natural skin, it will have kick marks, scars, soft pieces from the belly of the hide and spine marks. You are really looking for character in the leather and work out which piece of leather will work in which part of the bag,' he explains.

What next?

Designs are drawn up on paper first and then the leather is cut out with the paper pattern attached to it. The edges as shaved or pared down so that the leather isn't too bulky at the joins. First, you make up the outside body and handles, and then the pockets. Linings are made from suede, leather or fabric, and brass and nickel clasps and catches are used to close the bags.

How long does it take?

A beginner will need the best part of a week to make a bag. Experienced leatherworkers will often be working on several bags simultaneously, so it's difficult to say how long it takes.

Where can I see Irish-made leather goods?

Craft fairs are probably the best place to see a range of handmade leather goods. Some leatherworkers also sell their products directly from their studios and offer occasional demonstrations in leatherworking. Garvan de Bruir at De Bruir Aviation Luggage has a beautifully-designed workshop on the Monasterevin Road in Kildare, where he welcomes visitors. See www.aviationluggage.com or Tel:087 6182290 for more details.

SIGN UP

The Holden Leather Company near
Dingle, County Kerry (Tel:066:9151796,
www.holdenleathergoods.com) gives five-
day, hands-on workshops in designing and
making handbags. Open to beginners and
those with some experience, participants
will be shown a range of styles and work
alongside craftspeople in the workshop
and the course includes follow up technical
support for those keen to continue
working with leather.

Another leatherworker, Cathy Prendergast,
is also planning to start courses in leatherwork as part of the Louth Creative
Community Hub in Dundalk, County
Louth. See www.louthcraftmark.com for
more details of her handmade bags, belts
and other leather goods. Roisin Gartland
gives occasional workshops in making
leather bags, gloves and other leather
clothing at her studio in the Design Tower,
Grand Canal Quay, Dublin 2 (Tel:087
2490984, www.roisingardland.com).
The Crafts Council of Ireland website,
www.ccoi.ie, has details of people
working with leather in Ireland.

BUY MATERIALS

Most leather used by Irish leatherworkers is
imported into this country in large quantities. It's best to ask the craftsperson
working with leather if they can sell you a
small amount to get started.

METALSMITHING

What is it?

Metalsmithing involves annealing copper, brass, bronze, silver or gold – that is, heating it until it is red hot and then allowing it to cool before hammering it into shape. A gas torch is used for annealing and the metal may need to be annealed several times while a piece is being worked on. The key difference between a metalsmith and a blacksmith is that the blacksmith hammers ferrous metals (iron and steel) into shape when hot, while the metalsmith hammers non-ferrous metals (copper, brass, bronze, silver or gold) into shape when cold. Metalsmiths may also be called silversmiths, goldsmiths or coppersmiths, depending on the principal metal they work.

Copper was the earliest metal used by humans. Simple stone implements were used to hammer this copper into shape. Later, people discovered they could melt copper using charcoal and later still, they realised that copper could be mixed with tin to form bronze, a harder, more durable metal. The Bronze Age heralded the beginning of a long evolution of metalworking techniques. Bronze was first used for making tools, weapons and decorative items. Metalworking techniques such as engraving were used in Egypt as early as 2,000 BC. The art of inlaying one metal into another metal to develop a contrasting colour was perfected in Japan, where it was used to decorate Samurai swords.

During the 1200s, metalsmithing became more mechanised as artisans began to harness water power. Guilds were also established during this time. Precious metals were first imported in large quantities into Europe during the fifteenth century. The word metal comes from the Greek metal-lon, meaning metal or mine, and today metals are mined all over the world.

What do metalsmiths make and what tools do they use?

Metalsmiths make everything from bowls, goblets, cutlery, teapots and coffeepots to trophies, chains of office and all kinds of jewellery. They use hammers of various sizes and small anvils or stakes to hammer onto, as well as soldering torches and polishing brushes.

What do the experts say?

There are various simple and advanced techniques that metalsmiths use to make objects. According to Brian Clarke, an experienced metalsmith who holds regular metalsmithing classes in his workshop in County Wicklow, the first techniques a beginner will learn are sawing and filing the metal into simple shapes. 'I teach people the basics of silversmithing over four days. In that time, they will learn how to heat and form metal through the annealing process. They will learn how to cut, file and solder a ring and set a stone into a round bezel on top of the ring. They will also learn how to make and solder a spoon with a handle and decorative end,' says Clarke.

MICHAEL McCRORY

BRIAN CLARKE

KEVIN O'DWYER

17

How long does it take?

A beginner will need about a day to make a spoon or a ring. An experienced metalsmith will take less time of course, but it depends on the intricacy of each individual piece. Metalsmithing can be a slow process and requires patience when starting out.

Where can I see the work of metalsmiths?

The National Museum of Ireland – Archaeology in Kildare Street, Dublin 2 has a wonderful collection of Bronze Age gold and other metals, as well as great examples of early Christian metalwork. The National Museum of Ireland – Decorative Arts, Collins Barracks, Benburb Street, Dublin 7 has an extensive collection of silver from the medieval period, but also features work by contemporary Irish silversmiths. The Hunt Museum, Rutland Street, The Milk Market, Limerick City has a significant collection of boxes, urns, jewellery and religious objects made from various metals. See the Crafts Council website, www.ccoi.ie, for contact details of silversmiths working throughout Ireland.

SIGN UP

Brian Clarke runs silversmithing classes for beginners and those with some experience in his workshop in Ballinaclash, Rathdrum, County Wicklow throughout the year. He also runs occasional workshops in more advanced techniques in his Wicklow workshop and in Autignac, Herault, France. See www.silversmithing-workshop.com or Tel:086-3432907 or 0404 46385 for details. Silversmithing is one of the skills taught at the Centre for Environmental Living and Training in Scariff, County Clare on their Weekend in the Woods introductory courses (Tel:061 640765, www.celtnet.org).

Silversmith Seamus Gill gives occasional classes in traditional silversmithing techniques from his studio in the Design Tower, Grand Canal Quay, Dublin 2 (Tel:01 6775701, www.thedesigntower. blogspot.com). Da Capo Goldsmiths (letmeknow@dacapo.ie) and Breda Haugh (Tel:01 6705738) also run occasional jewellery design and making workshops from their studios in the Design Tower, Grand Canal Quay, Dublin 2 (www.thedesign-tower.blogspot.com).

BUY MATERIALS

Most tools required for metalwork are now bought online. However, many metalsmiths also source materials from Philip J. Dix, 6 Aston Quay, Dublin 2 (Tel:01 6717144, www.engraveireland.com). It's always best to check with the craftsperson who ran the course you attended before purchasing materials.

WORKING WITH GLASS

What is it?

Glasswork involves creating pieces that are functional, sculptural or both, using a range of different techniques. Those
who work full-time with glass usually either work with cold
or warm glass, or with hot glass (i.e. glass-blowing).

Glass has been used for thousands of years to make simple
containers and windows. Records suggest that glass beads
were first made in the Middle East about 4,000 years ago.
Glass-blowing was introduced in the first century BC.

The Egyptians and the Romans used glass extensively and glass craftsmanship – cut-glass work, gilding, enamelling and glass painting – developed in the first and second centuries AD. Initially, glass was mainly produced in the Middle East, China, India and Japan. However, by the early Middle Ages, glass skills had travelled West and the cathedrals and churches of Europe became embellished with brilliant windows depicting the saints and icons of Christianity.

By the fourteenth century, Venice had developed as a major centre of glass production. New centres also developed in Germany and Eastern Europe. In the nineteenth century, new developments made glass cheaper to produce and in the second half of the nineteenth century, extravagant glasshouses were built to house the Great Exhibitions in France and England. Designers in the Bauhaus movement in the 1920s and 1930s created designs incorporating suspended glass panels – the precursors of modern glass walled office buildings. In the twentieth century, glass workers throughout the world started to blend influences from East and West to create what are now known as modern glassworks.

How is it done?

Glass-blowing is really just for experts, although some studios will allow beginners to have a go. Glass-blowers start by shaping a blob of semi-molten glass on the end of a long hollow blowing iron. Then,

CATHERINE KEENAN

they blow into the cool end of the blowing iron and when the cool air strikes the hot glass, it forms a bubble. Sometimes, other layers of glass are added and melted into the piece at the mouth of a furnace. Then the pieces are blown and shaped further before being finally cracked off the iron and baked in the kiln for between twelve and twenty-four hours. Glass-blowers work with intense heat, which can be quite dangerous.

What about stained-glass pieces?

This is an easier process. It involves cutting up already-coloured glass and putting them back together with either lead or copper foil. You have to learn how to cut glass, how to solder it and you have to carefully consider your de-

sign. It is an easy enough process to learn but it takes time to perfect.

And fusing glass?

Fusing glass involves putting pieces of glass together and then firing them in a kiln so they join together. 'The important thing here is to choose pieces of glass that are compatible with each other, because if they expand or contract at different rates, they crack. The exciting part is that you put in raw sharp bits and get something out that's rounded and finished,' says Linda Mulloy from the Blue Glasshouse studio in Westport, County Mayo (www.blueglasshouse. com). Glass can also be melted into specific shapes in a kiln using ceramic or plaster mounds.

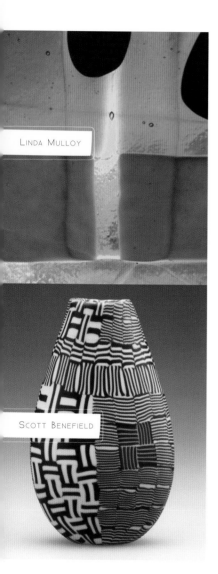

LINDA MULLOY

SCOTT BENEFIELD

How long does it take?

Different processes take different lengths of time. Blowing glass is a fine art that requires precision and care, but pieces are generally finished in a day and then fired overnight. Small stained glass pieces can be made in a day but the putty holding the glass into the lead needs a few days to dry. Fusing glass doesn't take much hands-on work but it needs varying lengths of time in the kiln. Building layers of glass or drawing on glass are additional techniques that demand more skill and time.

Where can I see examples of handmade glass?

The public can watch glass-blowers at work in the Jerpoint Glass Studio in Jerpoint, County Kilkenny from 10 AM – 4 PM, Monday to Thursday, and 10 AM – 1 PM on Fridays (Tel:056 7724350, www.jerpointglass.com). Similarly, visitors to the Kite Design Studio of the Irish Handmade Glass Company in Henrietta Street, Waterford can also watch glass-blowers in action (Tel:051 858914, www.irishhandmadeglass.com).

The National Museum of Ireland – Decorative Arts, Collins Barracks, Benburb Street, Dublin 7 has one of the best collections of Irish glass designed from the eighteenth century to the present day. Craft shops around the country also stock a range of handmade glass goblets, dishes and other decorative pieces. The Hunt Museum, Rutland Street, The Milk Market, Limerick City has a significant collection of stained glass panels, cut glass and blown-glass objects (Tel:061 312833, www.huntmuseum.com). Glassmakers also display and sell their work at craft fairs – the best of which takes place every December in the RDS, Ballsbridge, Dublin. The international trade fair Showcase, held in the same venue at the end of January each year, also includes a good range of contemporary glasswork. The Kilkenny Design Centre in Kilkenny city and on Nassau Street, Dublin 2 also sells some contemporary glass work. Contemporary examples of stained glass can be see in churches, hotels, museums and other public buildings throughout the country.

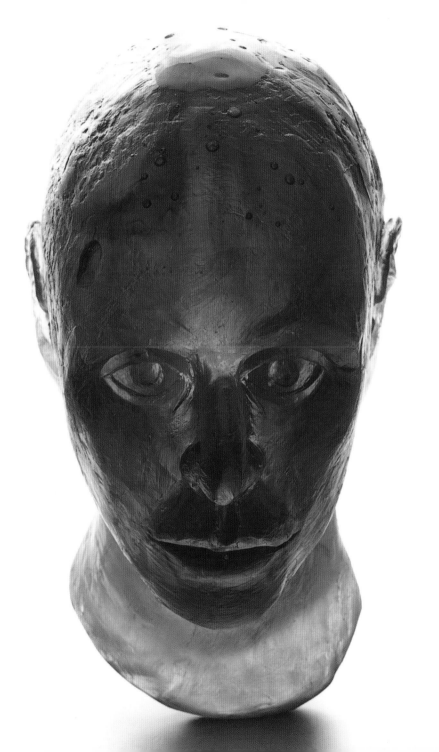

CAROLINE MADDEN

KILLIAN SCHURMANN

SIGN UP

The glass studio at Kerry Crafted Glass in Knockataglemore, Kilcummin, Killarney, County Kerry gives free introductory glass-blowing workshops from time to time (Tel:064 6643295), and Linda Mulloy holds stained-glass workshops for beginners and improvers at the Glasshouse studio in Westport, County Mayo (Tel:087 7981123, hotblueglasshouse@yahoo.co.uk). Pangur Glass Craft, in Drumroragh, Ballyjamesduff, County Cavan, runs regular workshops in glass-fusing (Tel:049 8545118, www.pangurbawn.com).

BUY MATERIALS

Dublin Art Glass at 62b Heather Road, Sandyford Business Park, Dublin 18 (Tel:01 2957261, www.dublinartglass.ie) and Pangur Glass Craft Supplies, 1 Lime Tree, Drumroragh, Ballyjamesduff, County Cavan (Tel:049 8545118, www.pangurbawn.com) supply tools and glass for those working with glass.

WOODTURNING

What is it?

When you turn wood, you create an object using a lathe – a machine that lets you shape the piece of wood by spinning it against a cutting tool. It has become a very popular hobby in recent times, as lathes can be bought quite cheaply and it's fairly easy to learn how to make basic functional pieces.

Woodturning has been practised since at least the sixth century BC and possibly for several hundreds years prior to that. The Etruscans (who lived in what is now Northern Italy) had well-developed turning techniques, and many examples of their work (wooden platters, beads, etc) from the sixth century BC have been found through excavations. Flat wooden dishes with decorative rims have also been found in Turkey.

Simple lathes used for turning wood are believed to be the first machine tools. Until the beginning of the nineteenth century, the tools for turning wood were handheld, then with the implementation of steam power, the metal cutting lathe developed rapidly.

Today, many of the items traditionally made from wood – domestic utensils, farm implements, musical instruments etc., are now machine-made. However, hand-turned objects, whether functional or ornamental, are treasured in homes throughout the world.

What type of wood works best?

Generally speaking, timber from hardwood trees is the best for woodturning. For example, an object turned from ash or beech will be more durable than one turned from pine. Woodturners will usually cut wood into planks along the length of the tree and then cut these planks into chunks. The shading and grain of the wood defines the finished piece.

How it is done?

There are several stages to the process. First and foremost, you have to find the

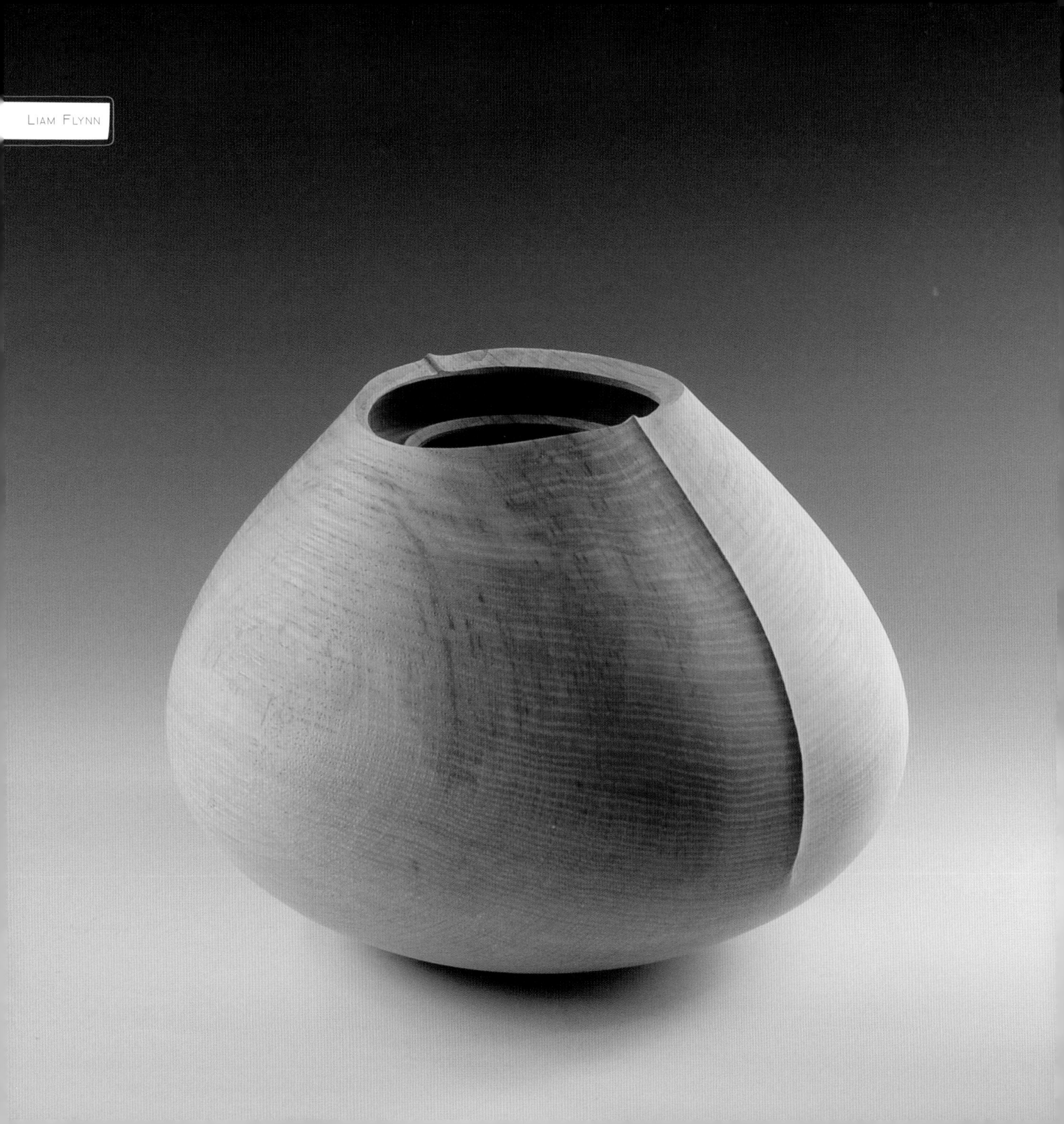

Roger Bennett

Glenn Lucas

right piece of wood. Professional wood-turners keep a stock of seasoned or dried wood ready to work on. They also often respond to offers of wood from recently-felled or fallen trees. Some dry their wood for six to eight weeks in a kiln, while others leave it for years to air dry. Amateurs can buy pre-dried timber to work on. Once you've chosen your piece of timber, you rough-turn it on the lathe to create the general shape and size of the piece. Next, you leave it to dry for up to ten weeks in a kiln, or much longer if air-dried. Then, you put it back on the lathe and turn it much more finely to create the final shape.

What do experts say?

'What draws people to turning is the love of the material and the speed you can shape a piece on the lathe. Some people will go home with several finished pieces after a day,' says Glenn Lucas, a County Carlow-based woodturner who gives regular classes. The key to good woodturning is to use very sharp tools, according to Lucas: 'there is as much to know about the correct sharpening of tools as there is to know about woodturning itself,' he says. Once you finish turning a piece, you sand it and oil it – with a food safe oil for functional pieces or with a high gloss oil for more ornamental pieces.

How long does it take?

It takes a professional woodturner about ten minutes to turn a salad bowl, whereas a beginner might take up to an hour. It's best to start with simple organic shapes and move on to more complicated pieces once you have gained some experience.

Where can I see examples of wood-turned objects?

Many woodturners sell their products in craft shops throughout the country. You can find a list of registered woodturners on the Crafts Council of Ireland website mentioned above. Some woodturners also sell directly from their workshops. Woodturners also display and sell their work at craft fairs – the best of which takes place every December in the RDS, Ballsbridge, Dublin. The international trade fair Showcase, held in the same venue at the end of January each year, also includes a good range of contemporary wood-turned objects. The Kilkenny Design Centre in Kilkenny city and on Nassau Street, Dublin 2 also sells the work of Irish woodturners.

SIGN UP

There is no official apprenticeship in woodturning so anybody who has a lathe and tools can teach the required skills. However, it's best to take classes from experienced woodturners and preferably those who are registered with the Crafts Council of Ireland (www.ccoi.ie). Glenn Lucas has produced two instructional DVDs on mastering the tools and techniques of woodturning (Tel:059 9727070, www.glennlucas.com).

BUY MATERIALS

Finding the wood for turning is the easy part. Basically, you need to look out for any trees that fall in your area (and check with the owners if they will give/sell you some pieces), contact local tree surgeons or saw mills. Glenn Lucas sells woodturning tools and occasionally sells lathes from his workshop in County Carlow (see contact details above), and you can also get tools from McQuillan Tools, Westend Retail Park, Blanchardstown, Dublin (Tel:01 8025100), Capel Street, Dublin (Tel:01 8733944) and 85 Oliver Plunkett Street, Cork City (Tel:021 4274990, www.mcquillantools.ie). Other tool suppliers include The Carpentry Store, Unit D4, M7 Business Park, Newhall, Naas, County Kildare (Tel:045 883088, www.thecarpentrystore.com) and The Wood Shed, 11 Lowtown Road, Templepatrick, County Antrim (Tel:44 (0)2894 433833, enquiries@wood-shed.com).

FURNITURE MAKING

What is it?

Much of the furniture we buy is made in factories abroad or assembled from parts made in factories throughout the world. However, there is also a small number of furniture makers working in Ireland, using traditional techniques to make unique and durable pieces of furniture.

How is it done?

Hand-crafted furniture begins with the selection of a piece of wood that inspires the furniture maker. This is particularly the case for items such as tables and cabinets, where the grain of the wood will feature strongly in the finished piece. Even for smaller pieces of furniture such as chairs and stools, the grain of the wood is crucial to the overall look of the piece. Following the natural grain of the wood also means that the furniture will be stronger and more long-lasting.

Garry Markham from Goose Island in Castlegregory, County Kerry makes chairs and stools using traditional construction methods and tools. He also offers two-day beginners workshops in stool making. The first thing to do is to split the log in half, then half again and again until you have the size you require. The advantage of splitting using hand-held tools (a froe and betal mallet) is that you keep to the grain of the wood.

Next, you pare the pieces down maintaining the strength of the grain. Larger pieces are prepared for the legs and arm posts, while smaller sections are kept for the spindles, which are shaved to almost finished size before drying them in a kiln.

You make the bows of the chair by steam-bending green wood or laminated seasoned wood. You start assembling the stool or chair when all the pieces of wood are dry. Then, it's sanded, French polished and oiled ready to last 100 years.

What do the experts say?

The time dedicated to each piece will depend entirely on the type of furniture required and the amount of detail in the finished piece. Tim Dunleavy, Kildare-based furniture maker says it took him about three weeks to make a cabinet recently. 'It could take twice that time. It really depends on the amount of detail the piece has and whether hand techniques – for example dove tail joints in a drawer as opposed to a machine joint – are used,' he explains. Tim Dunleavy and his brother, Sean use a combination of traditional and modern techniques to make their individually-commissioned tables, cabinets, chest of drawers, chairs and other pieces..

Where can I see examples of handmade furniture?

You can see examples of bespoke furniture at workshops of individual furniture makers. These include Garry Marcham at Goose Island Workshop in Castlegregory, County Kerry (Tel:066 7139896, www.gooseislandworkshop.ie) and Dunleavy Bespoke in Caragh, Naas, County Kildare (Tel:087 2738814, www.dunleavybespoke.com). Check out other furniture makers on the Crafts Council of Ireland website, www.ccoi.ie.

You can also see pieces of handcrafted furniture by Irish furniture makers at Showcase, the international craft, gift and fashion trade fair held in the RDS, Ballsbridge, Dublin every January (www.showcaseireland.com).

THOMAS KAY

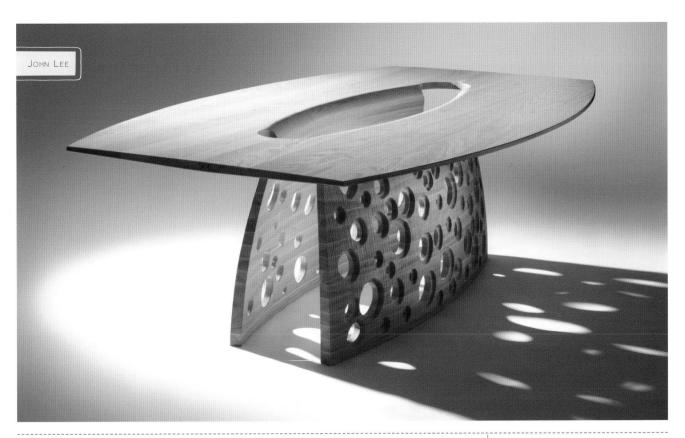
JOHN LEE

DUNLEAVY BESPOKE

CILLIAN JOHNSTON

SIGN UP

Woodwork and Construction Studies are popular evening courses held in Colleges of Further Education throughout the country. Check in your local library for details. Hill Picket Studios in Ballymurtagh, Avoca, County Wicklow run week-end, morning and evening courses in furniture making, as well as musical instrument making (Tel:0402-30581, www.hillpicketstudio.com). Goose Island Workshop (Tel:066 7139896, www.gooseislandworkshop.ie) run courses in stool and chair making. Pat Lawless at Lawless Furniture, Ballyferriter, Tralee, County Kerry gives occasional demonstrations in his workshop but more often gives workshops at music festivals such as Electric Picnic in Stradbally, County Laois (Tel:066 9156410, www.lawlessfurniture.com).

BUY MATERIALS

It's best to start by doing some basic courses in woodwork before buying tools or wood for making your own furniture. Some courses provide basic materials for making follow-up pieces, once the basic techniques have been acquired.

GOOSE ISLAND WORKSHOP

CRAFT IN FOCUS:
LATITUDES

Airfield, Dundrum, Dublin / Summer 2011
An exhibition featuring site-specific fibre art by the members of
Filament Fibre Artists. Events organised to coincide with the exhibition
included workshops associated with the Bealtaine Festival, National
Drawing Day and Airfield's own 'Family Sundays'.

SHEILA JORDAN: FORMATION

HILARY BELL: ROCK SOLID

MATERIAL MEMORIES: LUCINDA JACOB/FAMILY WORKSHOP

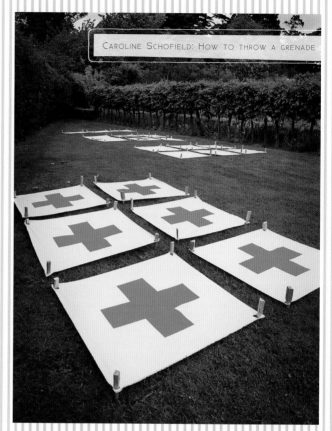

CAROLINE SCHOFIELD: HOW TO THROW A GRENADE

JEAN MCKENNA: FRACTURED LIGHT

MARY HEFFERNAN: TEMPTATION

TARA NÍ NUALLÁIN: YOU ARE HERE

STITCHING AND WEAVING CRAFTS

JUDY CINNAMOND

EMBROIDERY

What is it?

Embroidery is the delicate art of stitching onto woven cloth. Traditionally, decorative stitches of different coloured threads were sewn onto patterns drawn or printed on the cloth. Historically, wooden stamps of flowers and birds were used to print the pattern onto the material. Nowadays, patterns are often transferred onto cloth using carbon paper.

Embroidery dates back to medieval times when ecclesiastical garments and fabrics, ladies gowns, bed hangings and much more were embroidered. Embroidery was so well regarded in Ireland one thousand years ago, that under Brehon Law, there was a fine of one ounce of silver for theft of an embroidery needle.

Many Irish laces – particularly Mountmellick work – are forms of embroidery and the expansion of embroidery ran parallel to the growth of the linen industry. In the mid-nineteenth century, more than one quarter of women were paid for embroidery work they carried out in their homes. And while embroidery lost its niche in the twentieth century, the skills of embroidery continued to be passed on to girls in convent schools throughout the country until about the 1980s.

Since then, interest in embroidery has become more specialised for amateur and professional textile artists. For example, some people specialise in making embroidery samplers – originally used to demonstrate the various stitches, now valued for their artistic merit. Similarly, some fashion designers and fabric artists now incorporate traditional embroidery stitches into clothing designs and framed works. Contemporary embroidery techniques include adding various embellishments to cloth or canvas without using a pattern (freestyle embroidery), and painting on to the fabric.

How do you do it?

At its simplest, you need an embroidery needle, embroidery threads in various colours and a steady hand to stitch with. Sometimes, a frame is used to stretch the material and keep it taut while it is being worked on. Most people can teach themselves how to embroider but group classes can offer support and encouragement. At embroidery workshops, beginners can meet like-minded people, see their work and learn different stitches.

How long does it take?

According to Phil Stewart, a member of the Irish Guild of Embroiders, embroidery can be slow, methodical work, although the length of time required to complete a piece of embroidery depends entirely on how much embellishment your piece requires and how fast you work. Famous embroidered works such as the Ros

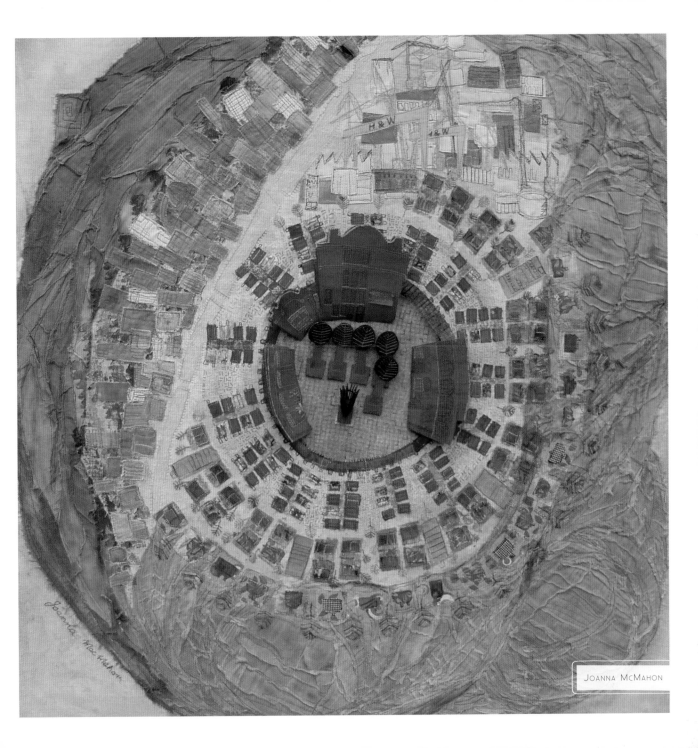

JOANNA MCMAHON

YVONNE WILLIAMS

Tapestry in Wexford and the Bayeux tapestry in France took years to complete. Incorrectly described as tapestries (which are, in fact patterns woven into the cloth on a loom), these famous works were made by several people who hand stitched the scenes onto cloth.

Where can I see embroidered works?

The Ros Tapestry, an incredible historic piece, created by many contemporary embroiders is on show in an exhibition centre, Priory Court, The Quay, New Ross, County Wexford (Tel: 051-445396, www.rostapestry.com). The Ulster Folk and Transport Museum in Cultra, Hollywood, County Down has a display of embroidery samplers (Tel:44 (0)28 90428428, www.nmni.com). Many smaller museums throughout the country also have displays of embroidery. The Mountmellick Museum, Mountmellick, County Laois (www.mountmellickdevelopment.com) has a permanent display of Mountmellick work (white embroidery on white cloth, sometimes called lace).

Embroidery artists and collectives of fabric artists hold occasional exhibitions of their work. See the Crafts Council of Ireland website (www.ccoi.ie) for details of exhibitions.

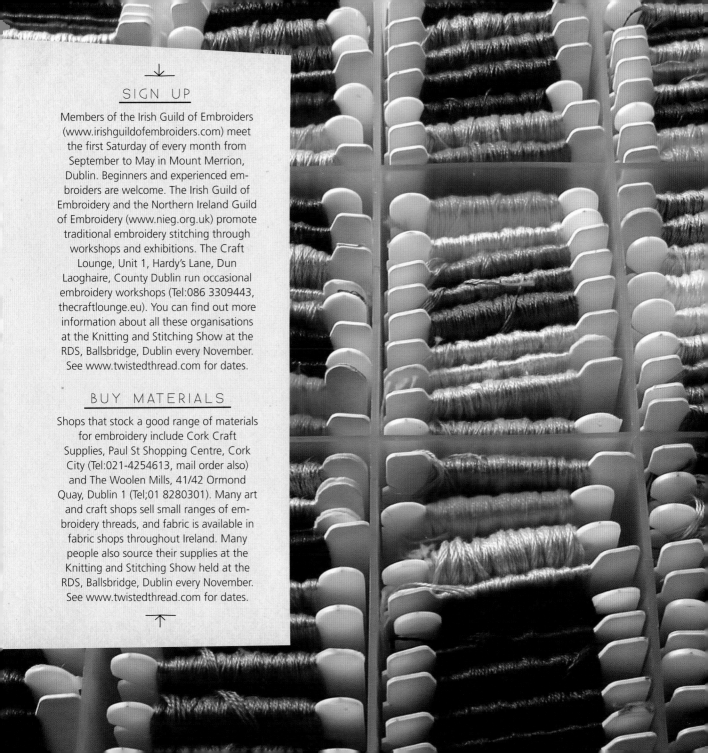

SIGN UP

Members of the Irish Guild of Embroiders (www.irishguildofembroiders.com) meet the first Saturday of every month from September to May in Mount Merrion, Dublin. Beginners and experienced embroiders are welcome. The Irish Guild of Embroidery and the Northern Ireland Guild of Embroidery (www.nieg.org.uk) promote traditional embroidery stitching through workshops and exhibitions. The Craft Lounge, Unit 1, Hardy's Lane, Dun Laoghaire, County Dublin run occasional embroidery workshops (Tel:086 3309443, thecraftlounge.eu). You can find out more information about all these organisations at the Knitting and Stitching Show at the RDS, Ballsbridge, Dublin every November. See www.twistedthread.com for dates.

BUY MATERIALS

Shops that stock a good range of materials for embroidery include Cork Craft Supplies, Paul St Shopping Centre, Cork City (Tel:021-4254613, mail order also) and The Woolen Mills, 41/42 Ormond Quay, Dublin 1 (Tel;01 8280301). Many art and craft shops sell small ranges of embroidery threads, and fabric is available in fabric shops throughout Ireland. Many people also source their supplies at the Knitting and Stitching Show held at the RDS, Ballsbridge, Dublin every November. See www.twistedthread.com for dates.

KNITTING AND CROCHET

What is it?

To knit, you use two needles and your fingers to guide the wool onto the needles. To crochet, you use one needle, known as a crochet hook, and your thumb and fingers to help you make each stitch.

All around the coast of Northern Europe, there are local knitting traditions and hand-knitting was introduced to Ireland in the 1600s. There were guilds of knitters in England in the middle ages and all members were men. In the late-sixteenth century, members of the guild furiously turned away the inventor of the knitting machine and he had to flee to France.

In Ireland, knitting schools were established throughout the country and knitting became a cottage industry and a welcome source of income for many households in the eighteenth century. The off-white coloured Aran sweaters with their detailed patterns are a symbol of Irishness throughout the world. Their intricate stitches and patterns continue to inspire contemporary fabric designs.

The word crochet is derived from the French, meaning hook. Some historians claim it dates back to practices in Arabia, China and South America however, the first references to its popularity in Europe are in the nineteenth century when machine spun cotton thread became widely available and inexpensive. Crochet patterns and instructions were published in the 1840s and crochet was particularly popular during the Victorian times but interest in it declined significantly throughout the twentieth century.

Despite this, some fashion designers in the early part of the twenty-first century have drawn inspiration from crochet. Crochet patterns also have an underlying mathematical structure and the craft has been used to illustrate shapes in hyperbolic geometry that are difficult to reproduce

KIERAN FOLEY

using other media and difficult to understand when viewed two-dimensionally. A hyperbolic crochet model of a coral reef has also been made to highlight environmental degradation of these beautiful underwater structures.

How is it done?

Nowadays, there are countless websites and youtube videos that you can learn to knit and crochet from. However, nothing beats that one-to-one contact. There are several skills to be learned in knitting: casting on (i.e. making) stitches; learning various types of stitches; increasing the number of stitches; decreasing the number of stitches; keeping the stitches evenly spaced as you knit and casting off the stitches at the end of the piece. There is a smaller variety of stitches to learn in crochet and the finished pieces can sometimes resemble lacework.

Children can learn to knit with large wooden needles and learn to crochet with a large crochet hook. Natural fibres (wool, silk, linen, cotton, cashmere and alpaca), or synthetic fibres (polyester, acrylic, viscose, rayon and nylon), or a mixture of both are used for knitting or crochet. Simple stitches and uncomplicated garments such as scarves are the best place to start.

How long does it take?

That depends entirely on what you are making. A practised knitter might take twenty-five hours to make a jumper for an adult, whereas a simple child's scarf might take about an hour.

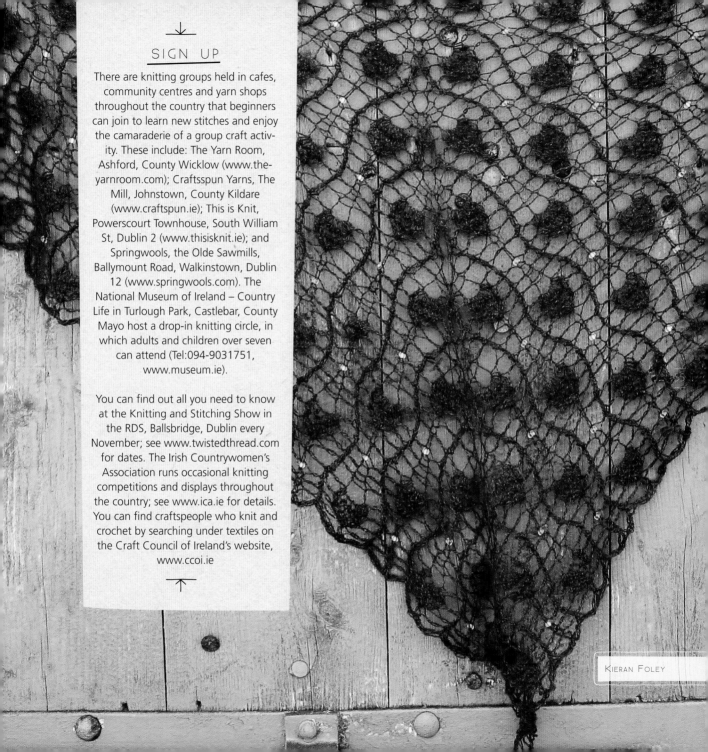

SIGN UP

There are knitting groups held in cafes, community centres and yarn shops throughout the country that beginners can join to learn new stitches and enjoy the camaraderie of a group craft activity. These include: The Yarn Room, Ashford, County Wicklow (www.the-yarnroom.com); Craftsspun Yarns, The Mill, Johnstown, County Kildare (www.craftspun.ie); This is Knit, Powerscourt Townhouse, South William St, Dublin 2 (www.thisisknit.ie); and Springwools, the Olde Sawmills, Ballymount Road, Walkinstown, Dublin 12 (www.springwools.com). The National Museum of Ireland – Country Life in Turlough Park, Castlebar, County Mayo host a drop-in knitting circle, in which adults and children over seven can attend (Tel:094-9031751, www.museum.ie).

You can find out all you need to know at the Knitting and Stitching Show in the RDS, Ballsbridge, Dublin every November; see www.twistedthread.com for dates. The Irish Countrywomen's Association runs occasional knitting competitions and displays throughout the country; see www.ica.ie for details. You can find craftspeople who knit and crochet by searching under textiles on the Craft Council of Ireland's website, www.ccoi.ie

KIERAN FOLEY

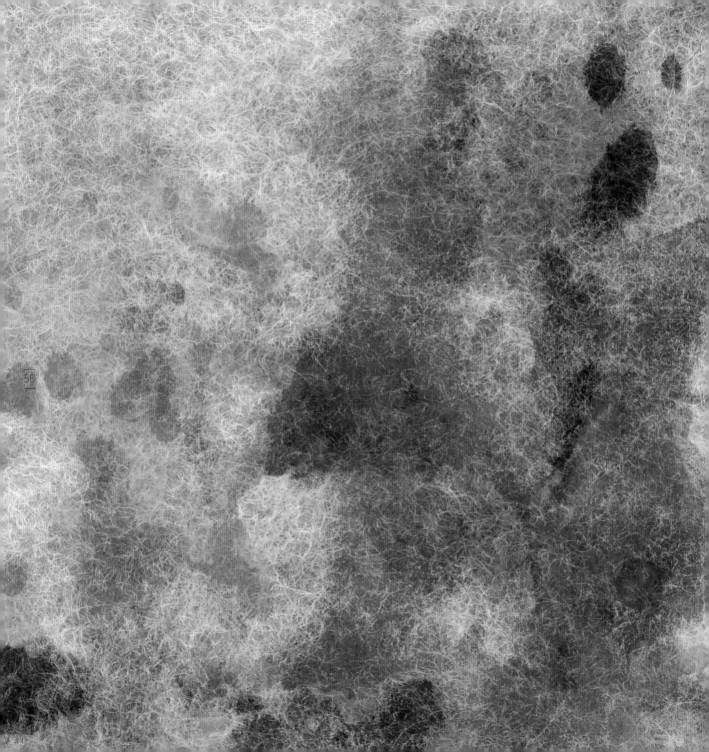

FELT MAKING AND BATIK

What is felt making?

You make felt by wetting and/or rubbing raw, unspun wool, which naturally binds together during this process to form the cloth. You can then use the felt to make bags, hats, scarves, babies' boots, other clothing or wall hangings. Felt is probably the oldest known textile.
Archeological findings from the Central Asian Steppes suggest that humans have been making felt from animal hair since at least 600 BC. The Mongols made their yurts or tents from felt. The basic principles of felt making remain unchanged to this day, as the essential ingredient is unspun wool moulded into shape with water, heat and friction. Nomadic peoples in Central Asia and northern parts of East Asia still make felt for their tents, rugs and clothes.

What is batik?

The word 'batik' means painted in Japanese. In batik, you decorate cloth by dying it after applying hot wax to certain areas. Then, when you remove the wax, the contrast between the dyed and un-dyed areas makes the pattern. Batik is a popular technique used for clothing, wall hangings and cushions.

In Ancient Egypt, mummies were wrapped in fabric patterned with wax-resist dyeing technique. In Asia, the technique was practised widely in Indonesia, Japan, China, India, Sri Lanka and Thailand, and certain tribes in Nigeria and Senegal used the technique to adorn their clothing.

The traditional colours first used in batik were indigo, brown and white, representing the three major Hindu Gods. Certain patterns could only be worn by nobility and a person's rank could be worked out by the clothes they wore.

Batik was introduced to Europe from the colonies and in the early 1800s, the Netherlands held the largest museum collections of Indonesian batik. Since then, it has become widely available and hand-dyeing techniques have largely been replaced by block-printing the wax onto the fabric. However, handmade batik remains a popular craft throughout the world. In 2009, UNESCO designated Indonesian batik as a masterpiece of oral and intangible heritage of humanity and the Indonesian administration has since asked its people to wear batik on Fridays to revive the industry.

How do you make felt?

There are two processes: Wet felting and dry-needle felting. For wet felting, you wash and untangle the wool, then place it in horizontal and vertical layers with bubble wrap on the bottom and top. You then gently massage it so that the fibres grip together and the wool matts and tangles naturally. Then, you can roll the whole lot up in a towel and roll it along a table.

For dye-needle felt, you put thick layers of wool on a foam block and punch down into the fibres with a strong needled brush. 'People are amazed that felt making doesn't involve stitching or weaving or gluing,' explains Sheila Jordan, a fibre artist. You can add raw silk fibre or silk fabric to the layers of wool to create different textures and colours. The process takes ten or fifteen minutes for a small amount of felt.

What is the technique for making batik?

You begin with a white or light-coloured piece of fabric, preferably cotton. You paint or drip hot wax into the shape or design you want. Then, leave it to dry for a few minutes. Next, you sponge or paint on a light-coloured dye and leave it to air dry. You repeat this process with more

wax and darker dyes until you are satisfied with your pattern. The last stage is to remove the wax. 'The piece of fabric will be very stiff so you can scrape off some of the wax with a knife and remove the rest by ironing the fabric between sheets of brown paper,' explains Janey Winchester, a textile and fibre artist. Waxing and dying cloth takes only minutes but the cloth has to be left to dry between layers.

Where can I see good examples of crafts made from felt and batik?

The Feltmakers Ireland website shows examples of its members' work, and at various workshops and courses held throughout the year; see www.feltmakersireland.com for details. The recently published book, *Profiles in Felt* features the work of forty-four felt makers in Ireland and has photographs of their work. The National Craft and Design Fair in the RDS, Ballsbridge, Dublin (www.nationalcraftsfair.ie) and the Knitting and Stitching Show (www.twistedthread.com) at the same venue are also good places to view work by feltmakers and batik artists. The website of Cork Textile Network (www.corktextiles.com) is another excellent place to view work by textile artists.

↓

SIGN UP

The Feltmakers Ireland website is the best place to
check for forthcoming workshops (www.feltmakersire-
land.com). Sheila Jordan gives felt-making workshops
from her studio in Kells, County Kilkenny (www.sheila-
jordan.ie); Nicola Brown also runs workshops from her
studio in Claheen, Borris, County Carlow (Tel:087
2789740); Janey Winchester gives batik and silk painting courses from her studio in Dunmanway, County
Cork (jpandkw@gmail.com); Tunde Toth, Arts
Practitioner also gives classes in contemporary and traditional batik techniques (tundetune@gmail.com).

The Craft Lounge, Unit 1, Hardy's Lane, Dun Laoghaire,
County Dublin (Tel:086 3309443, www.thecraft-
lounge.eu) also run felting workshops, as does the
Organic Centre in Rossinver, County Leitrim (Tel:071
9854338, www.theorganiccentre.ie). See the Craft
Council of Ireland's website, www.ccoi.ie, for details of
the various feltmakers and batik artists giving workshops and classes around the country.

BUY MATERIALS

The best place to start is to the contact Feltmakers
Ireland via their website, www.feltmakersireland.com.
As well as running classes and workshops, the organisation also sells wool fibre and gives good advice to
beginners on what they need to get started. The Yarn
Room in Ashford, County Wicklow is also a good shop
to buy materials. Similarly, the aforementioned Knitting
and Stitching Show in the RDS, Ballsbridge, Dublin is
also an excellent place to buy materials. Specialist art
and craft stores sell dyes and wax for use in batik. The
fabric can be purchased in any good fabric shop.

↑

PATCHWORK AND QUILTING

What is it?

Put simply, patchwork is the act of stitching together single pieces of fabric of various shapes and sizes. Quilting involves putting together this layer of patchwork with a layer of padding called wadding and a backing fabric. These terms are however, used interchangeably.

Quilted bedcovers were made in Europe from the 1500s and settlers from European countries brought the craft of quilting to the Americas, where it became widely established and continues to enjoy a particular prominence in some parts of the United States. In Ireland, decorative patchwork was introduced by women in large country houses in the eighteenth century who taught their servants needlework skills including patchwork and quilting.

Initially, patchwork and quilting were expensive pursuits because fabric was expensive. In larger, more well-off homes, patchwork quilts were made from discarded garments of silk, satin, taffeta and high velures. Then, as clothing factories were built in Ireland, it became associated with thriftiness. In poorer households, women used all kinds of cloth, including flour bags, whose mill could sometimes be identified on the backs of the quilts. The magic of patchwork is that cast-off materials can

be transformed into something new, unique and beautiful. Nowadays, quilting has become an art form and so-called art quilts are used as wall-hangings rather than on beds.

How is it done?

Traditionally, decorative patterns were created in symmetrical repeated blocks of hexagonal, diamond or square designs using templates. Metal templates were used to cut out cardboard shapes to insert into the patches initially to define the shape. You take the cardboard out once you have stitched the patches together. Like many crafts, patchwork requires both precision and patience as it can take a year or more to complete a patchwork quilt. Once the pieces are all stitched together, the padding and backing fabrics are added. The quilter will then add lines of stitching throughout the finished piece.

Contemporary quilts have more loosely designed patterns or pictures with pieces of cloth added on (appliqué). Various other embellishments such as crystals, beading, sequins and decorative stitching are also added to contemporary quilts. Whole cloth quilts are quilts made of a single piece of material and embellished with decorative stitching.

What do the experts say?

The length of time needed to produce a quilt will depend on the detail of the design and size of the piece. A fairly simple design on a patchwork quilt for a double bed could take between ten and twenty hours to machine stitch, whereas hand-stitched quilts could take over a year to complete. Despite such a lengthy commitment, hand-stitching a quilt can be a labour of love, as Mary Hunter from the Irish Patchwork Society suggests: 'Quilts bring memories of warmth, comfort and security. They are familiar objects, yet they carry hidden histories and untold stories about textiles, women's creativity and individual families.'

Where can I see examples of Irish patchwork quilts?

The National Museum of Ireland – Country Life in Turlough Park, Castlebar, County Mayo (Tel:094 9031755,

www.museum.ie) and the Ulster Folk and Transport Museum in Cultra, Hollywood, County Down (Tel:44 (0)28 90428428, www.nmni.com) have displays of historic and contemporary patchwork quilts. The Irish Patchwork Society and the Quilters Guild of Ireland also have occasional exhibitions of members' work. For instance, the Irish Patchwork Society will have a national exhibition of members work in Limerick in 2012. Contact the individual organisations for up-to-date information on forthcoming exhibitions.

SIGN UP

There are two principal organisations which promote quilting and patchwork in Ireland. The Irish Patchwork Society (www.irishpatchwork.ie) has about five hundred members in eight branches, who meet monthly in various venues around the country. The Eastern Branch meets in St Anthony's Hall in Clontarf, Dublin on the fourth Saturday of each month. The Knitting and Stitching Show in the RDS, Ballsbridge, Dublin 2 in November is a great place to meet members of the Irish Patchwork Society (www.twistedthread.com), who also gives introductory classes in patchwork for adults and children at the show. The Quilters Guild of Ireland (www.theqgi.com) promotes quilting and patchwork through newsletters and meetings. The Clew Bay Quilting studio in Gloshpatrick, Westport, County Mayo runs quilting workshops for beginners and improvers (Tel:098-64014).

BUY MATERIALS

There are several women who run home-based shops that sell everything you need to get started. These include: Patchwork Plus, Aghada Hall House, Lower Aghada, Midleton, County Cork (Tel:021 4662908); Fabric Matters, Dublin (Tel:01 4946420); Inspiring Ideas, Unit 417 Retail Park 2, The Blanchardstown Centre, Dublin 15 (Tel:01 8219277); The Sewing Shed, Castlemaine, County Kerry (Tel:087 9924002); Rags for Linda, Outherard, County Galway (Tel:091-550779); Threads of Green Fabrics, Purcellsinch Business Park, Dublin Road, Kilkenny (Tel:056 7762514); The Limerick Quilt Centre, Winander House, Park Road, Limerick (Tel:061 419790); Kilbora Quilt Shoppe, Kilbora, Camolin, Enniscorthy, County Wexford (Tel:087 6512109); and Farmhouse Quilts, Croneyhorn, Carnew, County Wicklow (Tel:053-9426344).

67

MILLINERY

What is it?

Millinery is the art and craft of designing and making a hat or headpiece. You could argue that the animal skins worn on the heads of cave dwellers were the first hats, as the principle of keeping the head warm and protected was surely what prompted people to make hats. Tomb paintings at Thebes show a man wearing a straw hat. Other early hats include the Pileus, a simple skull cap and the Phrygian cap, which later was called the liberty cap given to slaves in Greece and Rome when they were freed. The Pestasos from Ancient Greece is the first known hat with a brim.

Although women traditionally had their heads covered with kerchiefs, hoods, caps and wimples, it was not until the end of the sixteenth century that women's structured hats, based on those of male courtiers, were made. The word milliner – a maker of women's hats – is derived from 'Milaner', the merchants from Milan who sold feathers, flowers and trimming for hats in the sixteenth,

seventeenth and eighteenth centuries. During the first half of the nineteenth century, the bonnet dominated women's fashion. Later, other styles developed and hats became enormous and elaborated adorned. By the mid-1920s, women's hair was cut shorter and the cloche, which hugged the head like a helmet with a very small brim, became very fashionable. From the 1930s to the 1950s, New York – with its many European immigrants – became the world capital of millinery. In the 1960s, hats became less fashionable, as wigs and exotic hairstyles took over. However, in the 1980s and 1990s, there was a revival of millinery and hats and sculpted headpieces – especially for formal occasions – once again have become fashion statements. The international prominence of Irish milliner Philip Treacy has further enhanced the public's appetite for innovative, contemporary design.

How is it done?

Firstly, you must choose the material you will use to make your hat. Generally, hats

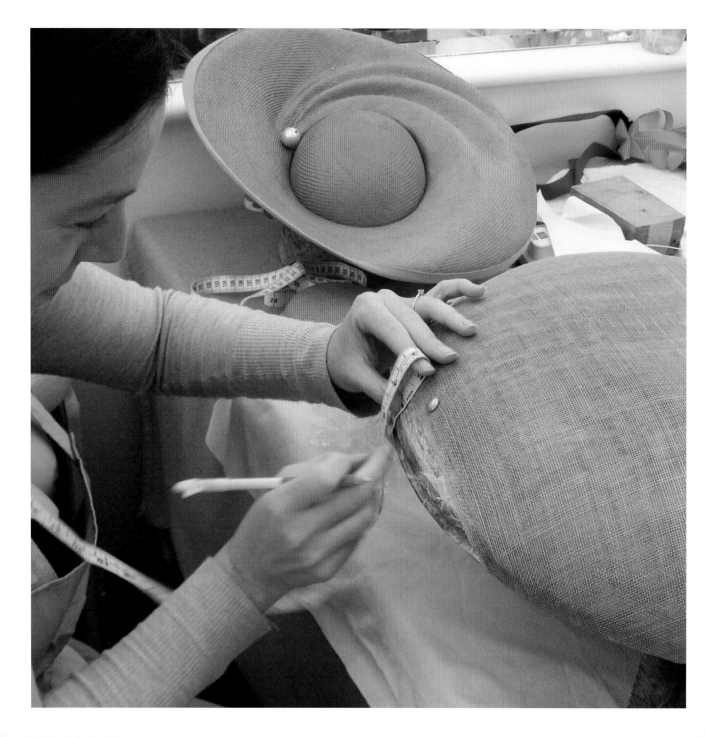

for the winter months are made from felt, while summer hats are made from straw or sinamay (a material made from palm leaf). Next, the material is moulded into shape on a wooden block. Felt is held over steam until it is soft and then it is pulled down onto the block; it is then left to dry overnight. The hat is stiffened by painting a chemical called shellac on the inside and left to dry again.

The hat is then trimmed into shape and wired along the edge. This wire is covered with fabric or ribbon binding. A length of millinery ribbon is sewn on the inside to act as a sweat band. Then, the hat is ready to be embellished.

What do the experts say?

Crucial to a successful headpiece is the hair band or a headpiece base upon which the design is built. 'The key is that it can sit firmly on the head and carry the weight of handmade flowers, leaves and veils,' says milliner, Linda McKay, who gives workshop in designing and making hats and headpieces. Embellishment is 'the never-ending part,' according to Lina Stein, who runs hat-making courses in County Mayo. 'You can add feathers, silk or velvet flowers, buttons, pearls, buckles, veiling. . .'

How long does it take?

Making the basic shape for the hat only takes a few minutes. It can take several hours then to add embellishments. A lot of time spent making a hat is waiting for something to dry. And generally, a professional milliner will be simultaneously working on three or four hats at different stages in the design process.

Where can I see good examples of handmade hats?

The major department stores in Dublin, Belfast, Cork and Limerick sell a good range of hats. Some small boutiques scattered throughout the country also specialise in hats. Milliner Marianne Flood displays her handmade hats annually at the Horse Show, RDS, Ballsbridge, Dublin and the National Crafts and Design Fair in the same venue (see www.rds.ie), as well as at Bloom, the annual gardening festival in the Phoenix Park, Dublin (www.bloominthepark.com).

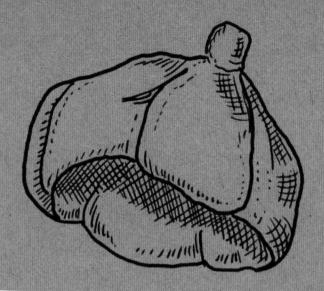

↓

SIGN UP

Lina Stein runs regular courses from her base near Westport, County Mayo and more recently in the Ennis Creative Arts Centre, Ennis, County Clare. Stein also runs three- and five-day intensive millinery workshops. Specific sewing skills aren't required; Stein says that all you need is to be able to thread a needle and put a button on (www.linasteinmillinery.com, Tel:098 28449).

Milliner Linda McKay runs one- and two-day workshops in making couture hats and headpieces from her studio near Inistioge, County Kilkenny. The one-day workshop is designed for those interested in making an individual headpiece to accessorise an outfit, while the two-day course will teach various skills in construction hats and headpieces (Tel:051 427991, www.lindamckay.ie). Rebekah Patterson gives introductory courses to groups at their own premises, or one-to-one classes from her studio in Kilkenny city.

BUY MATERIALS

Fabric shops are the best place to start. You can also get advice from those running workshops/classes in millinery. Find craftspeople who make hats by searching under textiles on the Crafts Council of Ireland website, www.ccoi.ie.

↑

LACEMAKING

What is it?

Lacemaking is the creation of intricate designs with fine threads stitched together using various techniques. It is a traditional craft, which originally only the very wealthy could afford to buy because of the many months of labour each piece required.

Lace was probably first imported into Ireland from France and Italy in the eighteenth century. Thread was also imported at this time to be used at bobbin lace centres in Lisburn and Bangor. Various orders of nuns developed lace rooms in their convents and taught young girls how to make lace, which was then sold throughout the world. For example, the

SHEELIN ANTIQUE IRISH LACE MUSEUM & SHOP

Sisters of Louis convent in Carrickmacross took over the organisation of Carrichmacross Lace over one hundred years ago and taught the craft to girls aged between eight and fifteen. Professional lace designs were also developed by artists at art colleges, and the Crawford School of Art in Cork was particularly renowned for its lace patterns. The techniques of making Irish crochet (lace made with cotton threads using a crochet hook) were also taught to men, women and children during the Great Irish Famine to provide a source of income for poor families.

More recently, the Royal Dublin Society craft competitions became the only official recognition for lacemaking in the country. However, many of the old lacemaking techniques have been revived and adapted in recent times and continue to provide inspiration to Irish and international fashion designers.

What are the different styles and techniques of lacemaking?

There are numerous styles and techniques used in lacemaking around the world. In Ireland, the principal styles are Limerick Lace, Carrickmacross Lace, Irish Crochet, Needlepoint Lace and Bobbin Lace.

For Limerick Lace, you use a needle and thread to stitch a design onto a toile or mesh cloth. You can also use a hook to pull the thread through mesh stretched over a tambour or circular frame. Embroidery stitches are

sometimes added as embellishments. For Carrickmacross Lace, you stitch the design onto fabric that you have fixed to the net, and then you cut away the unwanted fabric.

For Irish crochet – Clones Lace, for example – you use a crochet hook with very fine thread to make individual pieces of lace that you then stitch together. Needlepoint Lace, such as Kenmare and Youghal Lace, is made entirely with a needle and thread. For Bobbin Lace, you braid threads to form a pattern; the loose end of each thread is wound onto a bobbin (a decorative turned stick with a spangle on the end to tension the thread) to make the threads easier to handle.

What kind of motifs might you incorporate into the designs?

Although in contemporary design, motifs have moved away from the more traditional roses and shamrocks, to incorporate other images such as leaves, acorns and flowers, lacemaking motifs are still largely inspired by nature.

What do the experts say?

You would need about an hour to make two centimetres of lace, according to Mary Shields, a lacemaker from the Guild of Irish Lacemakers who gives classes in Ireland and abroad and recently spent

over 300 hours making a lace fan for her daughter to carry at her wedding. Professional lacemakers make everything from christening robes to wedding gowns and contemporary designers also make pieces to frame or hang on the wall.

Where can I see examples of Irish lace?

The most comprehensive collection of Irish lace is on permanent exhibition in the Sheelin Irish Lace Museum in Bellanaleck, County Fermanagh (Tel:44 (0)28 66348052, www.irishlacemuseum.com). Permanent exhibitions of lace can be seen in the Carrickmacross Lace Gallery, Market Square, Carrickmacross, County Monaghan (www.carrickmacrosslace.ie), and in the Kenmare Lace and Design Heritage Centre (www.kenmarelace.ie). The National Museum of Ireland – Decorative Arts in Collins Barracks, Dublin has the national collection of Irish lace however, it is not currently on exhibition.

SIGN UP

The Guild of Irish Lacemakers holds regular meetings in Dublin. New members can join the guild and then sign up for classes. Classes are held throughout the year in Carrickmacross Lace, Mountmellick Work (which is technically embroidery but was traditionally called lace where it originated), Bobbin Lace, Irish Crochet and other styles. Day-long meetings of the Guild are often held on Saturdays (Booking enquires to Imelda Kelleher on Tel:087 2211618). Lacemakers in Carrickmacross (www.carrickmacrosslace.ie), Cork (www.traditionallaceireland.com), Clones (www.cloneslace.com) and Kenmare (www.kenmarelace.ie) also run classes.

BUY MATERIALS

The best idea is to get in touch with members of the Guild of Irish Lacemakers (www.irishlace.org), who will give you advice on what materials to buy for different types of lacemaking. The Kenmare Lace & Design Centre in Kenmare, County Kerry also sells materials for making lace (Tel:064 66 42978, www.kenmarelace.ie). The Sheelin Irish Lace Museum has a museum shop attached to it, which sells antique lace (Tel:44 (0)28 6634 8052, www.antiqueirishlace.co.uk).

WEAVING

What is it?

Weaving is the making of fabric for wall-hangings, rugs, table mats, throws or items of clothing, by passing horizontal lengths of yarn (the weft) over and under vertical lengths of yarn (the warp) on a loom.

The earliest known evidence of woven material in Ireland dates from about 1,600 BC, as pottery from that period shows signs of woven material in which the clay was placed before firing. The National Museum in Kildare Street, Dublin has a fragment of cloth found in a bog in County Antrim dated from at least 700 BC.

Fragments of woven fabric and weaving tools have also been found in excavations of Viking and Medieval Dublin. The skills of weaving and spinning were so important in early Ireland that the Brehon Laws (written about 600-800 AD) lay down as part of a wife's entitlement in case of divorce, that she should keep her spindles, wool bags, weaver's reeds and a share of the yarn she had spun and the cloth she had woven.

Weaving in Ireland developed in two principal ways. Firstly, the rural handweaver, working in his own home (as looms developed men did the weaving and women did the spinning and dyeing of wool), supplied the needs of the neighbourhood. And, secondly, from the thirteenth century onwards, urban craftsmen developed a weaving industry for both the domestic and export market. However, according to the Irish Guild of Weavers, Spinners and Dyers, this industry was largely destroyed by restrictive laws imposed on the export of Irish woolen cloth in the late 1600s and didn't revive again until the late 1800s. However, during the eighteenth and nineteenth centuries, there was a thriving silk and poplin weaving industry based around the Liberties area of Dublin.

Early looms probably consisted of one main beam propped above ground level with warp threads strung independently,

SILK WEAVING

each weighed down with a stone. A loom with a horizontal frame and a reed to separate the threads was invented later and later still, heddles to separate groups of thread and a hand thrown shuttle were introduced. The fly shuttle was invented in 1733 and became popular in the nineteenth century for linen weaving. A loom incorporating a fly shuttle was introduced to County Donegal for woolen weaving and gradually replaced the throw loom.

By the twentieth century, there were power mills, handweaving mills and individual weavers operating throughout the country. The Irish Homespun Society was founded in 1936 but it wasn't until a later revival in the 1970s that the fledgling Irish Guild of Weavers, Spinners and Dyers came into being. The Guild continues to be the best source of information and inspiration for weavers, spinners and dyers and students of these crafts.

How it is done?

You can weave with a table-based or floor loom. Most people prefer floor looms because you can work with your feet, using pedals, as well as your hands. You can weave smaller pieces of tapestry on a timber frame.

What's first?

You begin by preparing the warp threads (the threads that run vertically from the top to the bottom of the fabric). You first have to decide how close you want these threads to be to each other and the total width of your piece, as well as deciding on the length of your warp. After winding the warp around a warping mill, you transfer it to the loom and spread out to the correct width. You then section off each thread with a raddle (a piece of wood with evenly spaced metal or wooden pegs) and feed it through the eyes of the heddles (pieces of string or wire that move the warp threads apart to allow you to weave the weft (the threads that run horizontally in the fabric) between them. The heddles are attached to the shafts and pedals which operate the loom.

What do the experts say?

Weaving can be tricky and you need to take care. 'If you don't have the threads evenly spread on the back of the loom, you'll have bad tension which will upset your whole piece,' says Muriel Beckett. 'The number of shafts and the order in which you thread the heddle and press the pedals will give you the variety of pattern.' Finally, you thread the warp through the reed (a finer raddle), which will keep your weaving in place as it develops. You feed the weft from side to side by winding it around a bobbin in a shuttle, which passes back and forth through the openings that the heddles create in the warp, thereby weaving the fabric.

What kind of yarn do you use?

You can choose between hand-spun or commercially-spun woolen, alpaca,

cashmere, linen, cotton or silk yarn. Some professional weavers spin and dye their own yarn; others will use commer-

cially-spun and dyed yarn, including manmade fibres such as acrylic nylon or metallic yarns.

How long does it take?

This depends on how much detail you put into the piece and if you add inlay (inserting shorter lengths of yarn in the weft). A professional weaver will make a scarf in about an hour. A beginner might need a day to make the same piece.

Where can I see good examples of hand woven fabrics?

The annual Knitting and Stitching Show in the RDS, Ballsbridge, Dublin is a great place to meet weavers and see them at work. The Irish Guild of Weavers, Spinners and Dyers exhibit and sell members' work, from small items such as hanks of hand-spun wool and handmade cards, to larger pieces such as wall hangings and floor rugs. Members also demonstrate spinning and weaving, answer questions and share information about weaving. See www.twistedthread.com for dates and opening hours.

You can also see handweavers at work in The Glebe Mill, Kilcar, County Donegal, Ireland. Mondays to Friday 9 AM – 5.30 PM and Saturdays 9.30 AM – 5 PM from May to October (Tel:074 973 8194, info@ studiodonegal.ie). Eddie Doherty is another handweaver who works on an

antique loom in his studio in Ardara, County Donegal (Tel:074 9541304, www.handwoventweed.com).

There are several museums which also explain the history of weaving. These include: the Irish Linen Centre & Lisburn Museum, Market Square, Lisburn, County Antrim (Tel:44 (0)28 92663377); the Ardara Heritage Centre, Ardara, County Donegal (Tel:074 9541704, www.ardaraheritagecentre.com); the Dun Lewey Heritage Centre, Dun Lewey, County Donegal (Tel:074 9531699, www.dunleweycentre.com) and the

Leenane Cultural Centre, Leenane, County Galway (Tel:095 42323).

There are also a number of working mills which are open to visitors. These include Avoca Handweavers, Avoca, County Wicklow (Tel:0402 35105, www.avoca.ie); Foxford Woolen Mills Visitor Centre, Foxford, County Mayo (Tel:094 9256756, www.foxfordwoolen-mills.ie); Kerry Woolen Mills, Beaufort, Killarney, County Kerry (Tel:064 44122, www.kerrywoolenmills.ie) and Magees, Ardara, County Donegal (Tel:074 9722660, www.mageedonegal.com).

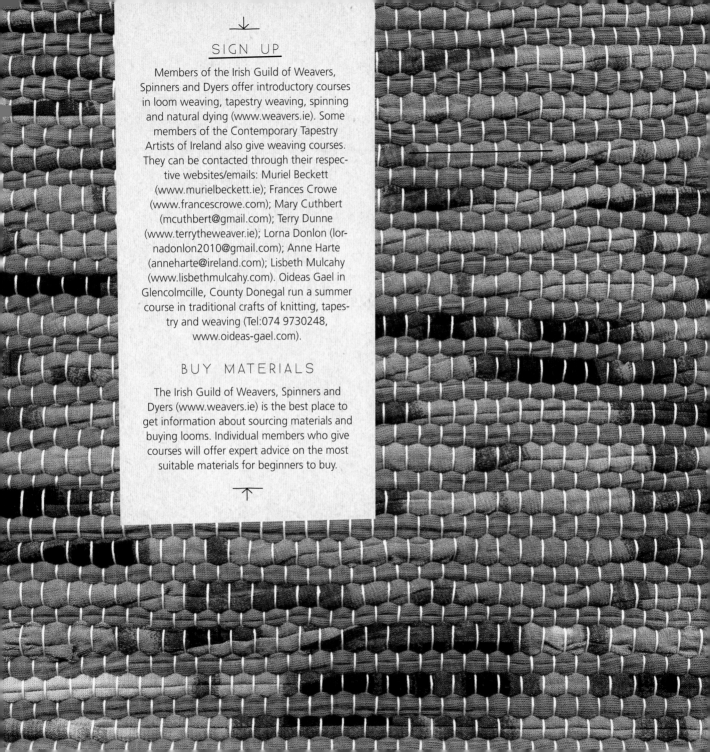

SIGN UP

Members of the Irish Guild of Weavers, Spinners and Dyers offer introductory courses in loom weaving, tapestry weaving, spinning and natural dying (www.weavers.ie). Some members of the Contemporary Tapestry Artists of Ireland also give weaving courses. They can be contacted through their respective websites/emails: Muriel Beckett (www.murielbeckett.ie); Frances Crowe (www.francescrowe.com); Mary Cuthbert (mcuthbert@gmail.com); Terry Dunne (www.terrytheweaver.ie); Lorna Donlon (lornadonlon2010@gmail.com); Anne Harte (anneharte@ireland.com); Lisbeth Mulcahy (www.lisbethmulcahy.com). Oideas Gael in Glencolmcille, County Donegal run a summer course in traditional crafts of knitting, tapestry and weaving (Tel:074 9730248, www.oideas-gael.com).

BUY MATERIALS

The Irish Guild of Weavers, Spinners and Dyers (www.weavers.ie) is the best place to get information about sourcing materials and buying looms. Individual members who give courses will offer expert advice on the most suitable materials for beginners to buy.

CRAFT IN FOCUS:

CRAFTED CREATURES

The Ark – A Cultural Centre for Children, Dublin / Spring 2011
An animal-themed exhibition of Irish craft curated by Brian Kennedy
and featuring the work of twenty-eight contemporary craftspeople.
The exhibition was specially commissioned by The Ark and the Crafts
Council of Ireland.

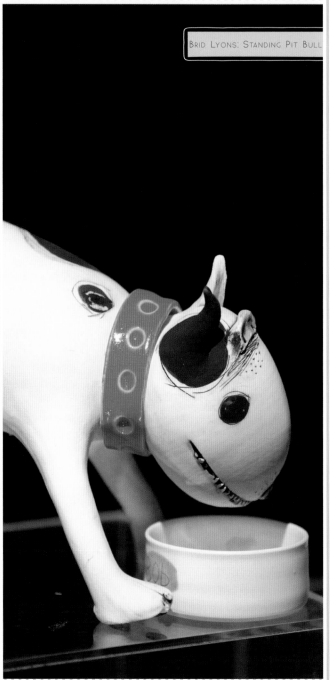

ee hens
rma, Sa ay and
heir co eal,
nning nd
aurs.
– KRYSTYNA P

Lian Callaghan: Hound's Play

Bob Johnston: The Brown Bull of Cooley

Prophet Moth
Lepidoptera Inspiration

HOME-BASED CRAFTS

MAKING BUTTER AND CHEESE

How is butter made?

Butter making is a simple process in which soured cream is churned or whipped until it separates itself into butter and buttermilk. The butter is then washed repeatedly and stored. Traditionally, butter was made in a churn and there were several different types of churns used. However, you can make a small quantity of butter by simply whipping sour cream with an egg whisk or even a fork. Alternatively, you can shake it in a jar with a tightly closed lid.

In rural Ireland, butter was made and sold at country markets by farmers' wives until the 1970s. Decorative wooden stamps were used to identify different farmhouse butters and also to make the butter look attractive on the table. You can see samples of these beautifully decorated wooden butter stamps and traditional butter churns at the National Museum of Ireland – Country Life, Turlough Park, Castlebar, County Mayo or at the Irish Agricultural Museum, Johnstown Castle, County Wexford (www.irishagrimuseum.ie). Homemade butter is still made and sold at markets by a small number of farmers.

How is cheese made?

Cheesemaking is a biological process which turns milk from a cow, sheep or goat into soft or hard cheese, using a cheese culture. When you leave milk in a warm place, it will naturally separate into curds and whey. When you put the curds and whey into a muslin bag so that the whey drains away, you will be left with a soft cheese. Cheesemakers use a starter or culture – lactic acid bacteria from animal rennet or microbial rennet produced by fermentation – to separate the milk into curds and whey.

Farmers who use their own milk for cheesemaking will mix evening milk with

Imen McDonnell

milk from the next morning to make cheese. Half evening and half morning milk is the traditional recipe for cheddar cheese. Raw or unpasteurized milk is also preferred by many cheesemakers. 'I have been making cheeses from raw cow's and goat's milk for the last twenty years and most of the award-winning Irish farmhouse cheeses are raw milk cheeses,' says Hans Wieland, who gives courses in cheesemaking. Many artisan cheesemakers oppose the current drive to ban raw milk in the EU (see www.irishcheese.ie).

Once you have curds and whey, you begin to cut or break up the curd. The size of the curd particles determines the type of cheese you can make. Smaller particles will produce harder cheese such as parmesan, while bigger particles will result in softer cheeses. The curd is then either washed, heated or simply left in the whey, again depending on the type of cheese you want. Next, it is separated from the whey and packed and pressed into wooden, steel or plastic moulds.

The cheeses are left in their moulds for six to twelve hours, then washed again in a salt bath and put on the rack to dry. They are then stored on wooden boards to ripen for a minimum of three to four weeks.

Cheese has been made from cow's and goat's milk as far back as 6,000 BC. Egyptian tomb murals from 2,000 BC show cheese and butter being made. Cheesemaking evolved in two main ways – liquid fermented milks and the acidification process which separates curds from whey. The Romans embraced and spread cheesemaking throughout Europe during the Roman Empire. Larger Roman houses had separate rooms for making and storing cheese. Tribes such as the Helvetica settled in the Swiss alps and developed their own distinctive cheese. Cheesemaking became very popular in countries such as Holland and France, moving from farm to factory in the nineteenth century. The process of pasteurisation meant it could be kept for longer and transported further. Processed cheeses took over from farmhouse cheeses in the 1950s, but from the 1980s onwards, farmhouse cheeses have been making a comeback; as evidenced by the growth of farmhouse cheeses in Ireland.

Where can I find homemade butter and farmhouse cheeses?

Some delicatessens and specialist food shops carry a range of Irish farmhouse cheeses. Farmers markets (see www.bordbia.ie for countrywide listings) and country markets (www.country markets.ie) are also a good place to source these products. The Irish Agricultural Museum at Johnstown, County Wexford has displays on traditional butter making with some beautiful butter stamps (Tel:053 9184671, www.irishagrimuseum.ie). The National Museum of Ireland - Country Life, Turlough Park, Castlebar, County Mayo also has a display on making butter (Tel:094 9031755, www.museum.ie).

SIGN UP

Hans and Gaby Wieland run courses in cheesemaking at the Organic Centre in Rossinver, County Leitrim (Tel:071 9854338, www.theorganiccentre.ie). Their two-day courses deal with hard and soft cheeses, fresh herb cheeses, yogurt and cheese in oil. The Irish Seed Savers Association, Capparoe, Scariff, County Clare, run various courses in cheese and yoghurt making (Tel:061 921866, www.irishseedsavers.ie).

Teagasc also run occasional cheesemaking courses for farmers who want to begin to make cheese; see www.teagasc.ie. You can see historic examples of the tools used in traditional cheese and butter-making at the National Museum of Ireland – Country Life, Turlough Park, Castlebar, County Mayo (Tel:094 9031751, www.museum.ie).

STORING AND PRESERVING
VEGETABLES AND FRUIT

What is it?

Storing and preserving your own fruit and vegetables means you can store the food you grow yourself, or buy cheaply when they are in season, and have them for the rest of the year. Before the invention of the freezer, storing and preserving food was a matter of great importance. There were all kinds of methods and storage containers used. By the nineteenth century, nearly all houses had walk in larders or pantries for storing food. Fish and vegetables were laid directly on cool stone or marble shelves and covered in muslin, while meat or game were hung in meat safes. Earthenware crocks and other glass and stoneware containers were used to store dry goods such as flour, sugar, salt and spices. Herbs were stored in paper bags.

Fruit was sometimes kept in nets and apples were either dried (cored and strung to the ceiling in nets) or laid out on shelves in a cool, dry loft. Kilner jars (which are still available today) were used to store soft fruits, berries and pickled vegetables.

In his incredibly detailed book, *The Forgotten Arts and Crafts*, the late John Seymour criticises the ubiquity of the deep freezer. 'It has meant that the art of bottling is now practically lost,' he wrote. 'This is sad, as tomatoes, plums, straw-berries and other soft and mushy fruit taste infinitely better bottled than frozen.'

In his chapters on kitchen crafts, Seymour also describes how icehouses were built and later replaced by the ice box, and he chronicles the emergence and dominance of the fridge and freezer. The methods of storing and preserving dealt with in this chapter draw on some traditional approaches that are now becoming popular again in some households.

How is it done?

There are several ways to store and preserve fruit and vegetables. The most popular ones are freezing, drying and storing in vinegar, oil or salt. Some people also store harvested vegetables in wooden boxes, on palates or in a hole between layers of straw and covered in dry soil. Carrots, for instance, are best stored in sand while apples can be laid out one by one (clean but unwashed) on palates.

Drying is the oldest preservation method and is suitable for vegetables, fruit, herbs and mushrooms. The process of drying has to be as fast as possible and the dried food has to be kept in an airtight container. Ireland isn't warm enough for air or sun-drying so food must be cut and placed on greaseproof paper in an oven at 65-75 degrees Celsius. Once cooled, they are stored in airtight containers.

For freezing, vegetables and fruit must be blanched first – dipped in boiling water and cooled immediately by plunging in ice cold water. They are then bagged and frozen.

Other methods include pickling in vinegar. This is most suitable for foods that are eaten in small quantities and taste well in vinegar, such as beetroot and small cucumbers. Some vegetables can also be preserved in oil. The most suitable ones for this method are those that are usually cooked in oil (e.g. tomatoes, mushrooms, artichokes).

Finally, fruits such as strawberries, raspberries, cherries, pears and plums can also be preserved in alcohol such as rum or other alcohol with honey.

How long does it take?

That depends on the method used and the amount of food that is preserved or stored. The most important thing to remember is that vegetables and fruit must be fresh, good quality and ripe but not over-ripe (except for drying, where over-ripe fruit is best). Containers must be clean and sterile. Everything should be carefully labelled and dated, and old or spoiled food should be discarded.

SIGN UP

Hans Wieland often gives a one-day course in storing and preserving vegetables and fruit and herbs at the Organic Centre, Rossinver, County Leitrim, (Tel: 071 9854338, www.theorganic-centre.ie). The Irish Seed Savers Association in Capparoe, Scariff, County Clare also run courses in storing and preserving fruit and vegetables (Tel:061 921866, www.irishseedsavers.ie). Courses are also held in Sonairte, The Ninch, Laytown, County Meath (Tel:041 9827572, www.sonairte.ie).

BUY MATERIALS

Storage jars, bottles and freezer bags can be bought in department stores and kitchen utensil shops. The oils, vinegars and alcohol can be bought in supermarkets and delicatessens.

MAKING WINE AND CIDER

What are the origins of wine?

In his book, *The Forgotten Arts and Crafts*, John Seymour states that wine has been made in every country in Europe where the sugar content of grapes is sufficiently high. References to winemaking have been found as far back as 6,000 BC in Iran and Israel. The Egyptians cultivated grapes along the River Nile. The Greeks and the Romans enjoyed wine and are probably responsible for spreading the art of winemaking across Europe. Traditionally, grapes were crushed with the feet so as not to break open the pips, which would spoil the flavour of the wine. The crushed grapes were then pressed to extract the juice, which was then simply left in a vat and allowed to ferment in its own yeasts. For red wine, the skins are left on and for white wine, they are taken off before fermentation.

How is wine made?

Although the wine that we buy is usually made from grapes, there is a long tradition of making wine from other fruits such as blackberries, gooseberries, elderberries or elderflowers. This is called country winemaking. Essentially, you make it by adding water, sugar and yeast to your chosen fruit. 'Grapes have the perfect blend of sugar, acids and tannins, which is the basis of a good wine,' explains Phil Wheal, who gives wine and cider-making courses. When you make wine from other fruits, you have to add sugar and wine yeasts.

The first step is to crush the fruit in boiling water (approximately 2 kgs of fruit to 4.5 litres of water). Then, add the sugar (approximately 2 kgs). Generally, the lighter the wine, the less sugar is added, and the stronger the wine, the more sugar is needed. Next you leave the mixture to cool until it is lukewarm (25 degrees Celsius), before adding the yeast and leaving it all to ferment for three to four days in a bucket covered in a cotton cloth.

What's next?

The wine is then filtered into demijohns – big bulbous bottles – and left for six to

eight weeks to ferment further, although this is an approximate time, and wines made from flowers or grains will take longer. When there are no longer any bubbles in the fermentation lock on the demijohn for about fifteen minutes, it's ready. The wine is drinkable at this stage but the flavour will improve further if it is poured into another demi-john and stored for a further few weeks in a cooler place. Finally, you bottle and store it until you're ready to use it.

There is a range of flavours you can produce from your own fruit, as Phil Wheal explains. 'Blackcurrants will produce a nice red wine, while gooseberries will give you a dry white table wine and elderflowers will give you a slightly medicinal white wine.'

What are the origins of cider?

When the Romans arrived in England, they were reported to have found local villagers drinking cider. Cider making be-came well established in Europe over the centuries and during medieval times, it was an important industry. Monasteries sold vast quantities of it and farm labour-ers even received a cider allowance as part of their wages. Its popularity proba-bly peaked around the seventeenth century, when every farm had its own cider orchard.

Traditionally, the apples for cider were crushed in a circular granite trough, around which a huge circular stone was trundled by a blindfolded horse. The crushed apples were then wrapped in strips of coarse hessian cloth to make what were called cheeses. These were laid out on planks under a press and great pressure was exerted on them – not once, but twice. The juice was then pumped into great casks – often as tall as houses – and left there to ferment. When ready, it was stored in wooden barrels.

Cider regained popularity in the twentieth century through mass production, but an interest in traditional cider making is currently enjoying a resurgence of sorts. Some cider makers add sugar or syrup to sweeten the cider for popular tastes.

What do the experts say?

To make a good cider, you will need a blend of dessert and cooking apples. You press the apples and add a cider yeast. 'Apple juice will naturally turn into cider if left to ferment with the wild yeasts, but you risk ending up with cider vinegar so it's best to use a cider yeast,' explains Phil Wheal. 'There are huge variations in cider making and numerous recipes but the key is to have the right mix of sweet and sharp apples,' he adds. As with wine, you will need to leave the cider to ferment for a few weeks before it is drinkable.

Where can I buy home made wines and ciders?

Some delicatessens and specialist food shops carry a range of wine and ciders from small producers. Farmers markets (see www.bordbia.ie for countrywide listings) and country markets (www.country markets.ie) are also a good place to source organic wines, and occasionally cider, produced for local consumption.

David Llewellyn gives courses in making cider in Sonairte, The Ninch, Laytown, County Meath (Tel:041 9827572, www.sonairte.ie). Phil Wheal gives courses in wine and cider making at the Organic Centre, Rossinver, County Leitrim (Tel:071 9854338, www.theorganiccentre.ie). Similarly, the Irish Seed Savers Association in Capparoe, Scariff, County Clare hold courses in country winemaking, cider making, as well as herbal beer making (Tel:061 921866, www.irishseedsavers.ie).

BUY MATERIALS

It's best to consult with those who run courses in wine and cider making about the best places to buy demijohns and other containers for fermenting wine and cider.

USING WILD HERBS IN COOKING
AND FOR MEDICINAL PURPOSES

Herbs have long been valued for their medicinal qualities and many modern pharmaceutical drugs are derived from plants or a synthetic derivative of healing properties discovered in plants. In the Middle Ages, monks planted herbs in their gardens and acted as physicians to the community. Herbs were also grown – sometimes very ornately – in manor houses of the Middle Ages and were prepared, dried and distilled for medicinal, culinary and scenting purposes. Kitchen herb gardens became popular in all homes and people grew culinary herbs, as well as herbs for making perfumes, ointments and pot pouri.

The introduction of spices from the East led to greater trade in spices and herbs, which eventually heralded the decline of the herb garden. However, the use of herbs for medicine and cooking by herbalists continued through the centuries, right up until the present time when it has become a degree subject in universities around the world. There has been a recent revival in interest among the general public in growing herbs and foraging for herbs in the wild.

What can I use them for?

Wild herbs are used in cooking, and herbalists also regard many of them – elderflowers, dandelion, hawthorn, silverweed, nettles, yarrow, comfrey and chickweed for example – as medicinal or therapeutic remedies. You must first learn where to find and how to identify each herb in the wild and then decide which part of the plant to use – flower or root or berry, for example. This generally depends on the time of the year you are foraging so for instance, you can pick elderflowers in May, and elderberries in September or October.

How do you use them in cooking?

You can add wild herbs to soups, salads, smoothies and stews. You can also use

COMFREY

wild herbs – fresh or dried – for teas and cordials. One way to store their leaves and flowers is to freeze them in small quantities in ice cube trays, ready for use in recipes as required.

How do you use them medicinally?

Many users of wild herbs believe in the adage, let food be your medicine so therefore consider the use of wild herbs in cooking as already useful to prevent infection and maintain good health. Herbalists use wild herbs in a range of remedies: for cough and cold remedies (elderberry syrup, for example), in blood tonics (the green tips of fresh spring net-tle leaves for example, and hawthorn berries or a tincture made from hawthorn flowers in springtime), as liver cleansers (dandelion root) and for relief of stomach and menstrual cramps (silver-weed).

What do the experts say?

'I believe in the prevention of illness by exploring wild herbs and keeping your-self nourished. Then, you can act on the first sign or symptom of an illness. Also the wild herbs that grow around you are the ones you need most,' explains Gaby Wieland, herbalist and naturopath.

112

SIGN UP

There are numerous day-long introductory courses on cooking with wild herbs and making your own herbal remedies. Naturopath and herbalist Gaby Wieland runs courses on Let Herbs Be Your Medicine in the Organic Centre, Rossinver, County Leitrim. (Tel:071 9854338, www.theorganiccentre.ie). Wieland also runs courses from her home in County Sligo and is willing to travel to give customised courses for groups of 10-12 people. Courses on foraging for wild food and cooking with wild food are also held in Sonairte, the Ninch, Laytown, County Meath (Tel:041 9827572, www.sonairte.ie).

Clare-based medical herbalist, Vivienne Campbell gives wild herb courses in the Irish Seed Savers Association, Capparoe, Scariff, County Clare, and runs herb walks in the Burren (Tel:086 8899168, www.theherbalhub.com). The Greenan Farm and Maze near Rathdrum, County Wicklow also run courses in wild foods and making herbal remedies (Tel:0404 46000, www.greenanmaze.com).

MAKING JAM AND CHUTNEY

What is it?

The art of preserving fruit in sugar or syrup is a very old tradition in Northern Europe where air-drying was not possible due to the colder climate. As sugar from the West Indies became cheap, jam making flourished and jam was made in most households throughout Ireland until recently. People ate a lot of jam on bread, scones, tarts and cakes. Now, the high sugar content of jam has made it unpopular. And, because fresh fruit is available all year round, the benefit of eating good-quality fruit preserved in this manner for winter consumption is no longer valued. However, as anyone who has tasted good quality homemade jam will testify, you can't beat it for flavour and texture.

Chutney is, quite simply, an alternative way of preserving fruit and vegetables to pickling. Rather than soaking the produce in vinegar, you boil it in vinegar. Chutney remains a popular accompaniment to cold meats and cheeses and more and more exotic fruity and spicy chutneys have become available in recent times.

How do you make jam?

Jam making has come back into fashion, in tandem with the Grow It Yourself movement and the revival of interest in foraging for wild foods. Although there's a relatively straightforward procedure to follow, you can end up with a syrup or a sauce rather than jam if you're not careful at each stage.

Firstly, you must choose fruit that is firm and ripe but not overly ripe. Overly ripe or damp fruit may stop the jam setting, or make it to go mouldy or ferment.

Generally speaking, jam is made with 1 kilogram of fruit to 1 kilogram of sugar, but when the fruit has a high pectin content – as blackcurrants do, for example – the jam will require less fruit. Pectin is the natural setting agent in ripe fruit. To start, you put the fruit in a large saucepan and simmer it very gently to extract the pectin and soften the skin or peel. Never add sugar until the skin or peels are tender and the stones have fallen out of fruits, such as damsons, as fruit will tend to toughen rather than become softer once you add the sugar.

Stir over a low heat until the sugar has dissolved and then increase the heat so the jam boils rapidly. Do not stir the jam as it boils as this can lower the temperature and prevent it from reaching setting point quickly.

Start testing the jam early to see if it has reached setting point, as over-boiling will produce either a jam that is too stiff or one that will never set. To test jam for setting, put a teaspoon of jam on a cold saucer and leave it to cool. If it wrinkles and feels firm, the jam is adequately set. If it's runny, leave it to boil for a little longer before testing again. Pour the hot jam into sterilised jars and cover immediately with circles of waxed paper. Leave it to cool slightly before sealing it. Store in a cool, dry and preferably dark place.

How do you make chutney?

Chutneys are a savory way of using up autumn fruits. The principal ingredient can be apples, beetroot or something more exotic like mangos (although these are still pretty pricey for homemade chutney). A typical apple chutney will contain about 1 kilogram of apples to 500 grams of brown sugar, 500 millilitres of water and 750 millilitres of vinegar. You can add onions, raisins, cloves, ginger and others spices and seasonings. To start, peel, core and chop the apples and put in a large saucepan with the water. Add chopped onions, raisins, ginger, cloves and sugar and simmer until soft. Add seasoning and vinegar and uncovered, simmer slowly until thick. Stir frequently to prevent the mixture from burning. Pour into warmed jars and cover at once.

Where can I buy homemade jam and chutney?

Jam and chutney are widely available for sale at local country markets and farmers markets. Some supermarkets, delicatessens and fruit and vegetable shops also stock locally-made jams and chutneys.

SIGN UP

You don't really need to sign up to a course to make your own jam or chutney; just follow a recipe carefully and enjoy. That said, various cookery schools throughout the country offer one-day or evening classes in jam and chutney making, so check out your local food directories for details.

115

MAKING SOAP
AND NATURAL COSMETICS

What are they?

Handmade soap and natural cosmetics are enjoying a resurgence of popularity in the last few years – partly as a reaction to the sometimes confusing diversity of mass produced cosmetics, but also due to the back-to-nature strand of the environmental movement gaining momentum throughout the world.

The origin of soap making lies in the humble open fire. You could say that humans have been making soap since primitive man discovered the lathering properties of animal fat mixed with wood ash, while cooking on an open fire. However, it wasn't for many centuries that soap became a household product. The Ancient Egyptians were more interested in painting their faces and developing the use of aromatic essences and herbs for embalming the

dead, and the Romans weren't too keen on soap either.

In the early and Middle Ages, using wild plants, vegetable and animal fats for household cleaners and ointments remained very much a home craft. However, artisans also began developing dying and soap making. Initially, soap was largely developed to prepare wool for dying rather than for personal hygiene.

By the thirteenth century, soap making had become established in Britain, France, Italy and Spain. The plentiful supply of olive oil in Mediterranean countries meant that olive oil was the principal ingredient, and places such as Castile in Spain and Marseilles in France became synonymous with soap making. In the Northern European countries, animal fats (tallow) were used.

Industrialisation brought the mass production of soap, and the combination of better soaps combined with advances in plumbing improved personal hygiene levels hugely. Soap remained a luxury until this time, after which it became more affordable and thereby available to everyone. Soap manufacturing thrived and the craft of making homemade soap all but disappeared.

However, in the last twenty years or so, people have become more interested in buying natural cosmetics and handmade soaps. The interest in learning how to make natural cosmetics came a little later – first amongst craftspeople and later among the general public. Weekend and day-long courses in making soaps and natural cosmetics continue to be popular, especially when participants can return home with gifts for family and friends.

How do you make natural cosmetics?

Natural cosmetics courses generally include making everything from lip balm to skin creams, toners, hair tonics, scrubs, face masks and cleansers, with separate courses in soap making.

There are different processes for different things. For example: you mash strawberries and yogurt with porridge oats or avocados with honey and essential oils to make face scrubs and face masks; for creams and lip balms, you add almond oil and essential oils to beeswax; Bread soda is the main ingredient of bath bombs; and for bath melts, you mix cocoa butter with dried flowers, such as lavender or rose. Skin toners and aftershaves are made from rose water or cider vinegar with essential oils.

How do you make soap?

Soap is the result of a chemical reaction between caustic soda which is strongly alkaline and oil or fat (which is an acid). Traditionally, the mixture of caustic soda and oil was stirred for a few hours but now, you generally mix it for about fifteen minutes with a hand blender, adding the essential oils and colours once the hardening process begins.

Then, you put the soap into moulds and leave it to set for a few days.

What do the experts say?

With natural cosmetics, 'face creams are the most complicated to make because you need to get oil and water to solidify with beeswax," explains Vivienne Campbell, a medical herbalist who runs courses in natural cosmetics.

Soap maker Anna Browne also advises would-be soap makers of the trickier elements to the process: 'It's important to match a precise quantity of oil – rape seed oil, vegetable oil, sunflower oil or olive oil – to caustic soda at the correct temperature because each oil has a different saponification (or soap-producing) value.'

Where can I buy natural cosmetics and soap?

The course providers mentioned overleaf also sell a range of natural cosmetics and soap. Contact them for more details. You may also find producers of natural cosmetics selling their products at craft fairs and farmers' markets throughout the country.

120

SIGN UP

There are several places to do workshops in soap making and natural cosmetics. Medical herbalist, Vivienne Campbell (Tel:086 8899168, www.theherbalhub.com) runs natural cosmetic courses throughout the country. Vanessa Finlow (www.verypure-soap.com) holds natural cosmetics workshops at The Craft Lounge, Unit 1 Hardy's Lane, Royal Marine Hotel, Dun Laoghaire (Tel:086 3309443, www.thecraft-lounge.eu), and at the Organic Centre, Rossinver, County Leitrim (071 9854338, www.theorganiccentre.ie). Soap making courses are also held in the Greenan Farm Museum & Maze, Greenan, Rathdrum, County Wicklow (Tel:0404 46000, www.greenanmaze.com)

BUY MATERIALS

It's best to ask those leading workshops for the best places to buy ingredients for making soap and natural cosmetics. Some will sell you small quantities of ingredients at the end of workshops.

CANDLE MAKING

What are they made from?

Candles are made from wax that has been melted and re-hardened. A wick is primed by being covered with melted wax, then carefully and steadily positioned in the centre of the mould or container, before the melted wax is poured into place.

The first candles were made by dipping a rush wick into fat, drawing it out for the fat to cool, then dipping it in again and so on until the required thickness was reached. Alternatively, the wicks were hung and hot fat was repeatedly poured over them. Occasionally, they were put into long rounded moulds with a small hole in the closed end. You poked the wick into this hole and poured in the fat from the other end and allowed it to cool.

When cotton was imported from hot countries, it replaced rush wicks. Over time, candlemakers also realised that if the wick was braided, it would burn better. Beeswax was the traditional wax used for candles in churches. Paraffin wax distilled from coal and oil shales was first made in the United States. The use of paraffin wax made candles cheaper and more available. Candlesticks, ranging from the simple chamber candlestick to more elaborate candelabra, were made to put candles in.

Although oil lamps gradually replaced candles from the 1700s onwards, they continue to be used in churches and

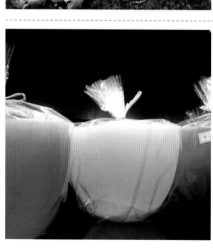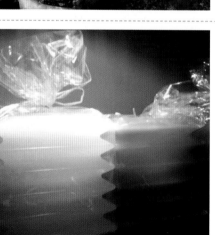

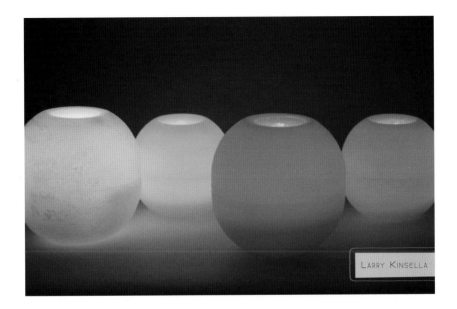

LARRY KINSELLA

homes for their atmospheric light in the evenings.

How is it done?

Candlemakers use a mixture of paraffin, vegetable or bees wax. Soy wax is also used by some candlemakers because it melts and burns at lower temperatures, gives off a cleaner flame and carries scent well. Stearin, or stearic acid, is added to the melted wax to prevent candles dripping excessively, and it also helps to make the wax opaque and to distribute colour. It prevents the wax smoking and makes the candles easier to remove from

moulds. Once the wax mixture is melted, the colour – in the form of soluble dye or pigment – and the scent are added. Scents used include essential oils, aromatic herbs and flowers. The melted mixture is poured into moulds of various shapes and sizes, ceramic or glass containers. Many candlemakers make their own moulds.

What do the experts say?

There are several methods to candle making. Some candlemakers prefer to melt large quantities of wax overnight at low temperatures, then pour the mixture into their moulds during the day and leave them to harden slowly. I use this approach because it makes the most of the colour, allowing the candle to glow and gives a textured finish,' explains Larry Kinsella of Moth to a Flame candles in Bennetsbridge, County Kilkenny.

Other candlemakers prefer to melt small quantities of wax, building up sections of coloured wax to create fun candles. 'I always work with small batches and build up colour in small batches too to make a variety of candles – including cupcake and sherry trifle candles,' says Fleur Daly of Bluebell Eco Candles, Market Lane, Killarney, County Kerry. To create layers of different colours, you must leave each layer to harden before adding another layer. It's important to remember that wax can never be melted over direct heat but must instead be heated in a saucepan over another saucepan with hot water.

Where can I see candles and historic candleholders?

The Ulster American Folk Park in Omagh, County Tyrone has a collection on lighting, which includes candles and candleholders. It also runs demonstrations in candle making (Tel:44 (0)28 82243292, www.nmni.com/uafp).

SIGN UP

Some candlemakers will demonstrate the process of candle making in their workshops. Fleur Daly of Bluebell Eco Candles runs candle making workshops for children aged eight to twelve, from April to September (www.bluebellecocandles.com). The Craft Lounge, Unit 1, Hardy's Lane, Dun Laoghaire, County Dublin run workshops in soy wax candle making (Tel:086 3309443, www.thecraftlounge.eu). You can also find candlemakers on the Craft Council of Ireland website, www.ccoi.ie.

BUY MATERIALS

You can buy candle making sets to make your own candles. Col Art Fine Arts and Graphics Ltd is a UK company that makes good quality candle making sets under the Dryad brand. Specialist shops such as Cork Art Supplies in Cork City (www.corkartsupplies.com) and Cregal Art, Monivea Road, Galway (www.cregalart.ie) sell wax, wicks, wick sustainers, dye and moulds for making your own candles.

124

FLEUR DALY

CRAFT IN FOCUS:

MODIFIED EXPRESSION

National Craft Gallery, Kilkenny / Summer 2011
An exhibition that featured an exciting mix of emerging and established artists whose work was inspired by the written word, or by the binding and recycling of books and paper, that responded to works from the literature strand of the Kilkenny Arts Festival.

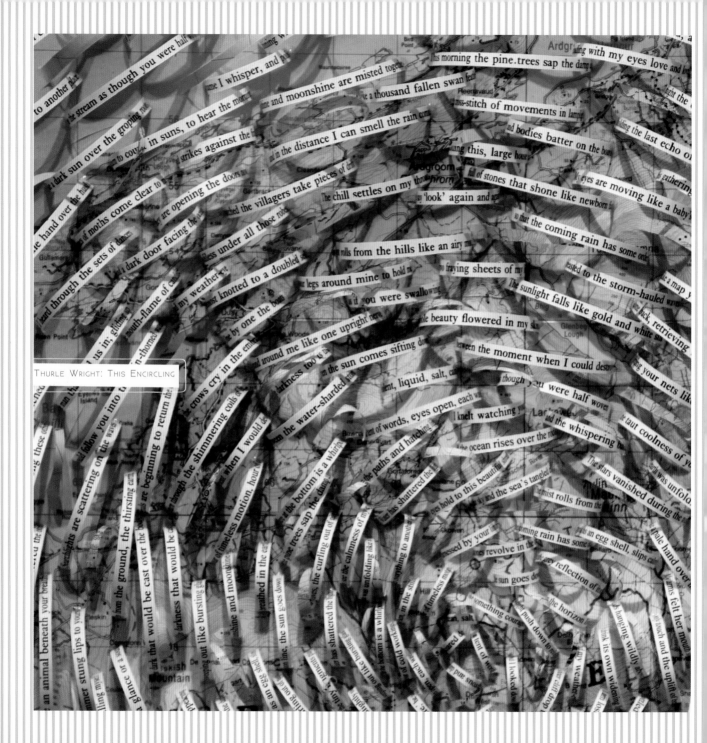

THURLE WRIGHT: THIS ENCIRCLING

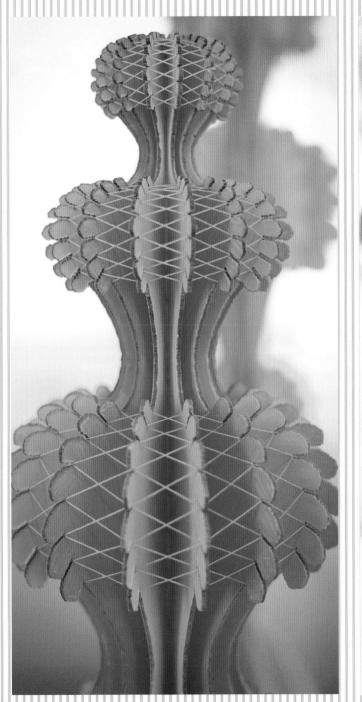

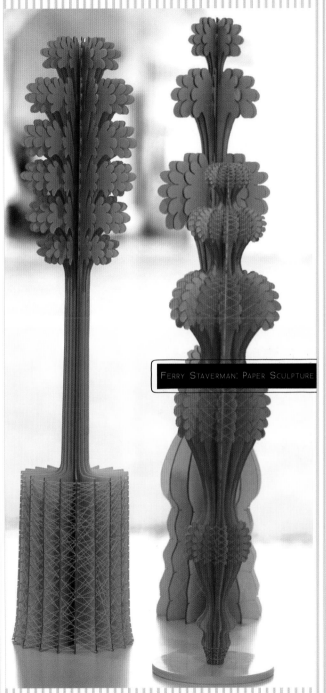

FERRY STAVERMAN: PAPER SCULPTURE

REBECCA COLES: THE WHITE BUTTERFLY

JOZEF BAJUS: THE STRAY SOD COUNTRY

BRIAN DETTMER: WE KILL ONE

JOZEF BAJUS: ELEGY FOR APRIL

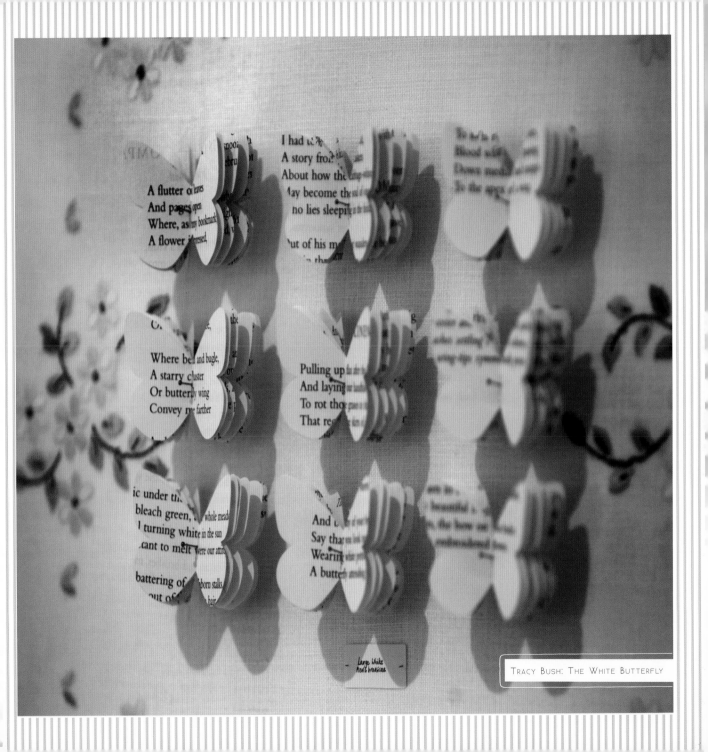

Outdoor Crafts

THATCHING

What is it?

Thatching is the art of roofing a house with straw, reeds or other natural materials. The first roof humans sheltered under – apart from the roof of a cave – was made of thatch, and the traditional huts of tribal Africans are nearly always roofed with thatch. The main difference between this form of thatch and European thatch is that the butts (bottoms) of whatever material is used is pointed downwards in European countries but upwards in Africa and Asia. In rural Ireland, thatching was the cheapest kind of roof there was, as most farmers could supply their own straw for the roofs. Thatched roof houses – one storey high – were the standard form of housing in rural Ireland until the early part of the twentieth century. From that time onwards, the thatch began to be replaced by corrugated iron, slates or tiles. Thatching skills are now required for the conservation of traditional style cottages owned privately or publically and occasionally, for roofing a new building with traditional features.

How is it done?

There are different techniques used in different parts of the country. Scolloped or pinned thatching is the most popular approach. You start by shaking out and laying a small bundle of straw neatly on the roof, ears end up and cut end down. You then pin this down on the roof with scollops (slender rods of willow, hazel or briars). You then get the next portion of straw and lay it a little higher up in such a way that it covers the scollops holding the first portion down, and so on until you reach the ridge of the roof. At the ridge, you bend the straw over and fasten it on each side with rows of scollops. The thatcher begins at the right-hand edge of the roof and works towards the left, completing a strip from eave to ridge, moving on until that side of the roof is complete. In the finished roof, the only scollops visi-

ble are those on each side of the ridge – often worked into a pattern – and at the eaves. In some areas, the first layer of straw is sewn directly to the roof timbers but nowadays, thatchers are more likely to use stainless steel screws to fix the thatch to the roof.

Roped thatch is another technique in thatching, which is more popular on the Atlantic coast in areas which are exposed to strong winds. In this approach, the thatch is held in position by a network of ropes rather than fastened directly to the roof. These ropes run over the roof and are fastened to the tops of the walls or to weights along the eaves.

What materials are used for thatching?

Traditionally, wheat straw was the most popular material used in most parts of the country. However, rye straw and oat

straw were also used and tough grasses or reeds were the materials of choice in mountainous districts. Flax or reed lasts for about twenty years, while straw will only last for between eight and twelve years. Nowadays, reed is the material of choice because it lasts the longest. Most of the reed used for thatching is imported from countries such as Turkey and Poland where there are large companies supplying thatch throughout the world. Smaller batches of Irish-grown reed is sometimes available on a more limited supply. Modern day thatchers also prefer to use reinforced steel, rather than hazel to pin the thatch to the roof.

How long does it take?

It takes about six weeks to thatch the roof of a forty-foot cottage.

Where can I see good examples of thatching?

Thatched houses can be seen dotted throughout the countryside, sometimes in unlikely places. However, they are most commonly seen in counties Mayo, Galway, Donegal, and Clare. The roped style of thatched roofs can still be seen on the Aran Islands – most notably on Inis Meáin. The hip-roofed style of thatched roof can be seen in Kilmore Quay, County Wexford. Clusters of thatched roof cottages still exist in North County Dublin (Rush and Skerries) and on parts of the Louth coastline (eg Clogher Head).

Thatched houses are a feature of Bunratty Folk Park, Bunratty, County

Clare (Tel:061 360788, www.shannon-heritage.ie) and The Ulster Folk and Transport Museum,153 Bangor Road, Cultra, Hollywood, North Down (Tel:+44 (0)28 90666630, www.nmni.com). The National Folklore Collection in the Newman Building, Belfield, University College Dublin also has information on the regional styles and materials used in thatching in rural Ireland (Tel:01 7168481, www.ucd.ie/folklore).
Thatchers give demonstrations of thatching at the Traditional Building and Conservation Skills in Action exhibition, organised annually in the summertime by the Irish Georgian Society. See www.igs.ie for details.

JIMMY LENEHAN

SIGN UP

Unfortunately, there aren't any courses currently available in thatching skills. However, a useful reference for thatching is the forthcoming Government publication: *Thatch - A Guide to the Repair of Thatched Roofs* by Dermot Nolan and Críostóir MacCartaigh (Architectural Heritage advice series).

BUY MATERIALS

The Irish Georgian Society's Traditional Building Skills Register is a good place to start to find experienced thatchers for advice. See www.igs.ie/resources.

DRY STONE WALLING

What is it?

Dry stone walling is building a stone wall without the use of lime mortar or cement.

Are all stone walls the same?

No, they vary hugely; from the single skin walls built with large smooth rounded stones, which are a feature of the Connemara landscape, to the herring-bone-style walls in County Clare, which are framed by large upstanding pieces of limestone. Depending on the regional availability of different kinds of stone, walls can be built from sandstone, limestone or even granite. The type of stone used influences the final look of the wall.

Dry stone walls have been a feature of the Irish landscape since the Stone Age. The Ceide Fields in north County Mayo, for instance, is the biggest European Stone Age settlement and is made up of dry stone walls. Dry stone walls continued to be used in Ireland even after lime became popular in other parts of Europe. They were popular in the nineteenth century as a barrier against soil erosion and to keep animals enclosed, and it is estimated that one quarter of a million dry stone walls were built in Ireland during this time. Irish people also brought their skills to Australia and the east coast of America when they emigrated there in the nineteenth and twentieth centuries.

How is it done?

To construct a dry stone wall, you must first grade your stones according to their size and shape as each stone will have a distinct purpose in the construction of the wall. Once the width of the wall has been measured and the trench dug, a so-called batter frame is placed on each end of the wall with pieces of twine running the length of the wall. The twine is moved during construction to help keep the wall straight, all the way to the top.

The largest, most awkwardly shaped stones are placed in the trench for the foundation of the wall. The next phase is the placing of the face stones on either side of the wall. Here, medium-sized flat-tish, almost square stones are best so that a brick-like structure can be built up.

What do the experts say?

The key to good dry stone walling is to use the largest stones for the base and work towards smaller stones as you build up. The real art lies in knowing which stone to lay your hand on next and how to place it. 'A good stone-waller will place a stone and pick up another to wedge it in place without ever dropping a stone,' says Richard O'Gorman, who teaches courses in dry stone wall construction. The centre of the wall is filled with rubble (smaller stones) called the

hearting. This process helps lock together both faces of the wall.

What next?

About two-thirds of the way up the wall, through stones (long stones that are the width of the wall) are placed at regular intervals along the wall. Then, smaller stones are placed on the top of the wall. These so-called coping stones are the important finishing touch to the wall.

How long does it take?

Experienced dry stone wallers will build a five-metre wall in about two days. Beginners can generally learn how to build a dry stone wall over the course of a weekend. Often, the walls are built in fields and gardens where the stone is already available. Sandstone is the stone of choice as it is easier to handle than limestone or granite.

Where can I see good examples of dry stone walls?

Ireland has one of the richest histories of dry stone walling in the world. The best place to see dry stone walls is on the Aran Islands, off the coast of County Galway. Counties Clare, Galway and Kerry also have plenty of examples of dry stone walls. Particularly impressive are the dry stone wall beehive huts on Skellig Michael, off the coast of County Kerry, and the oratory of Gallarus on the Dingle peninsula in County Kerry.

SIGN UP

Courses in dry stone wall construction are held at the Organic Centre, Rossinver, County Leitrim (Tel:071 9854338, www.theorganic-centre.ie) and at the Centre for Environmental Living and Training, Scariff, County Clare (Tel:061 640765, www.celtnet.org). Pat McAfee also runs courses in dry stone walling (Tel:087 2631872, mcafee@eircom.net), as does the Conservation Services in Marshallstown, Kilmessan, County Meath (Tel:046 9431040, www.conservationservices.ie).

BUY MATERIALS

Many quarries sell and deliver various grades of stone for dry stone wall construction. To match local landscape tones and to reduce emissions from unnecessary transportation, it's best to source stone locally.

HEDGE LAYING

What is it?

Hedge laying is the art of partially cutting hedgerow trees near the ground and bending them over (i.e. laying) to form a hedge. New growth comes from the cut stumps which rejuvenate the hedge, thicken up the base and prolong the life of the hedge indefinitely. A well-laid hedge provides a living barrier to sheep and cattle and a habitat for wild birds, plants and insects.

Hedge laying was commonly practised in Ireland until the 1950s. There has been a recent revival of interest due to the Rural Environmental Protection Scheme and environmental groups such as the Hedge Laying Association of Ireland. The hedge laying season runs from the beginning of September to the end of February.

What plants are in hedgerows?

Hedgerows are ideally made up of varieties of indigenous Irish species. If you choose to freshly plant a hedge, it is recommended to use about 70 percent whitethorn mixed with a variety of plants including holly, ash, spindle, dog rose, blackthorn, oak and hazel.

How it is done?

Hedges are laid either to rejuvenate an existing boundary hedge, or to make an old hedge stock proof again. The first task of the hedge layer is to clear dead wood, weeds and to cut back any growth that is not needed when you lay the hedge. This process is called clearing out and facing off the hedge. The stems are then partially cut at an angle as close to the ground as possible and bent over.

What do the experts say?

'Hedge laying is like major surgery to the plant and the key is to have these stems thin and flexible enough to bend and not break,' says Andy Booth, a trainer in hedge laying. 'Five to ten new shoots will

come up from the base or stump and these will be the stems to be laid again in thirty to forty years time,' explains Booth.

What's next?

Stakes are put in place fifty centimetres or so apart to support the interwoven branches of the hedge. In some places, hazel rods are braided together along the stakes at the top of the hedge. This is not a very common technique in Ireland, but it can look nice and gives great strength to the hedge. It is recommended that farmers fence off newly-laid or planted hedges for a few years until they are strong enough to be a stock proof barrier. Hedges should then be maintained in an 'A' shape, preferably cut only on one side each year and cut a little further out each time.

How long does it take?

A professional hedge layer will lay thirty to thirty-five metres of hedge in a day. Beginners can learn the basic principles of hedge laying in a one-day course. The tools required for hedge laying include a bill hook, a spar hook, a pruning saw, a rake and a wooden mallet. A chainsaw will, of course, speed up the process greatly.

Where can I see good examples of hedge-laying?

Demonstrations of hedge laying take place occasionally around the country, see The Hedge Laying Association of Ireland website, www.hedgelaying.ie, for details.

The Hedge Laying Association of Ireland (HLAI) has a number of certified trainers in hedge laying on its website, www.hedge-laying.ie. The HLAI has also produced a DVD on hedgerow management.

One HLAI trainer, Andy Booth (www.conservationservices.ie) gives beginners' courses in hedge laying in Sonairte, The National Ecology Centre, Laytown, County Meath (Tel:041 9827572, info@sonairte.ie).

BUY MATERIALS

The Hedge Laying Association of Ireland sells bill hooks and can also give advice on the purchase of other hedge-laying tools. Regarding the planting of hedges themselves, it's best to check with the person running the course you are attending as to what plants are the most appropriate.

↑

147

WHITETHORN

BOATBUILDING

What is it?

Traditional boatbuilding involves making boats by hand with timber as a key material.

Two separate strains of boatbuilding developed historically: the Mediterranean-type boats used by the Egyptians and southern European countries evolved from the currach, while the Nordic people developed boats from dugout canoes. According to boatbuilder Del Harding, these two traditions met in Ireland. The Viking ships came across the North Sea to Scotland, and then around Northern Ireland to Galway. Meanwhile, the Mediterranean-style of boat moved North towards Holland and worked its way around the South of Ireland to Galway. 'It is these boats that we refer to as Irish traditional currachs and hookers,' says Harding. Fishing boats made with wicker bottoms were also used until the 1840s along the west coast of Ireland, and later in rivers.

The availability of fibreglass moulds led to the decline in traditional boatbuilding from the mid-twentieth century onwards. However, there has been a revival of interest in building boats from timber in the last ten years or so. It is now generally acknowledged that fibreglass boats are just not as seaworthy as timber boats because they can't grip the waves in the same way.

How is it done?

How you build a boat depends on what it is going to be used for. Many of Ireland's lake boats follow the Viking tradition of using long single planks. These overlapping planks are nailed through and then thin strips of timber are steamed and bent into shape for the ribs of the boat. This is called the clinker-style of boat.

To construct what's called a carvel-style boat, the ribs are carved out of solid timber using the natural form of the wood. The skeleton of the boat is built first and then the planks are added later. Different types of timber are used for different parts of the boat, depending on the type of pressure anticipated and the type of curve required.

A group of skilled boatbuilders could build an average-sized lake boat in about a month. An individual boatbuilder might take several months to build a boat.

What do the experts say?

Traditional boatbuilder Del Harding likens the structure of a boat to an animal. 'There are several stages and essentially, a boat is built on a natural structure much like a skeleton and a skin. A boat is all curves because a curve is the natural shape required for buoyancy and friction-free movement through the water. This is very important because the pressures are from the outside and the water can move in any direction,' he explains.

Where can I see good examples of hand-built boats?

Most timber boats are built for private customers. However, you can see historic examples of currachs in some folk parks and museums. The National Museum of Ireland – Country Life, Turlough Park, Castlebar, County Mayo has a display on traditional boats (Tel:094 9031755, www.museum.ie).The pre-historic park in Craggaunowen, Kilmurray, Sixmilebridge, County Clare has a display of the leather-hulled, currach-style boat, built by Tim Severin for his historic sailing across the Atlantic, re-enacting the voyage of St Brendan and the early Christian monks reputed to have discovered America centuries before Columbus. See www.shannonheritage.com for more details.

WOODBOFIN

WOODBOFIN

SIGN UP

The Centre for Environmental Living
and Training (CELT) run summer
courses in traditional boatbuilding. The
aim of the eight-weekend-long course
is to foster the use of traditional skills,
as well as teaching the fundamental
principles of boat design and execution. More details can be found on
www.celtnet.org or Tel:061 640765.
Traditional wooden boatbuilding
courses and workshops are also held in
West Cork and Limerick through the
not-for-profit organisation AK Ilen
(Tel:086 2640479, www.ilen.ie).

BUY MATERIALS

As with furniture making, it is probably
best to start by doing some basic
courses in boatbuilding before buying
tools or wood for building your own
boat. Course providers are the best
people to advise you on the materials
required and where to purchase them,
as well as what tools you should
buy/rent to do the job.

WORKING WITH HORSES

What is it?

Before the invention of the tractor, horses were used to plough and harrow the land for sowing crops, to remove stones from fields, to spread manure, to cut and save the hay or haul timber from woodlands. People in Ireland relied on horse power until well into the twentieth century and in many other parts of the world, the use of animal power is still a day-to-day reality. It is estimated that there are about 500 million working animals used throughout the world.

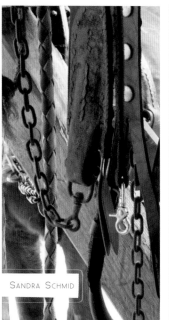

SANDRA SCHMID

Recently, there has been a revival of interest in using horses on farms in Ireland. Some farmers, particularly organic farmers with small acreage are considering draught horses. In France, an organisation in the South of France started promoting modern horse-drawn farm equipment in 1991 and now produces a full range of equipment for market gardening, horticulture and use in vineyard and fields. In the UK, the working horse is also making a comeback and timber extraction by horse has been a growth area over the last twenty years. The National Trust, for instance, regularly employs horse loggers, and some local authorities are also using heavy horses for park maintenance, rubbish clearance and plant watering. There are also a lot of work horses used in the United States of America.

What do the experts say?

The Irish Work Horse Association trains people in the practical skills of working with horses on the land. 'People think working with horses is just for nostalgia but using a horse for farm work is practical for people who have a small holding. Horses don't compact the soil and damage woodlands in the way that machinery will,' says Sandra Schmid, who uses two Irish cob horses on her farm in West Cork.

Basically, you need to learn how to handle horses while on the ground. 'What's new for people who ride horses is exactly this: learning how to walk behind or between a horse and a farm implement. You need to think safety all the time and use your voice rather than your legs to control the horse,' says Sandra Schmid. Work horses learn how to respond to voice and get used to pulling. Various exercises are used to train the horse to get used to movements on his back and learning how to stop and go and turn around when required to do so. 'Working with horses looks easy but it's very complicated and to do it well requires a lot of practice and patience with yourself,' adds Schmid.

What breeds of horses are trained as work horses?

Traditionally, Irish draught horses were used on farms, but over time, these horses have become lighter as their role has changed. Some farmers now use gypsy cob horses (traditionally used by Irish Travellers for pulling caravans), Clydesdales, French breeds such as Percherons or the Belgian Ardennes.

Where can I see people using work horses?

Working horse demonstrations now take place at various agricultural shows around Ireland. These include the Kingdom County Fair at Ballybeggan Race Course, Tralee, County Kerry; The South East Clare show in Bridgetown, County Clare and The Bantry Agricultural Show in Bantry, County Cork in September. See www.irishworking-horseassociation.com for full details.

SIGN UP

Sandra Schmid runs day-long and weekend courses in working with horses on a small holding near Bantry, County Cork (Tel: 087 9389867, www.horsepowerinireland.com). Forthcoming courses will teach skills of working with horses and horse-drawn tools, as well as training a horse to work with a harness and do logging work. Jim Cronin gives hands-on practical courses in harnessing, driving and using machinery on his farm near Bridgetown, County Clare (Tel:061 372685). Christophe Mouze gives courses in working and driving horses on Clare Island, County Mayo (Tel:098 25412, www.ecofarm.ie), and the Irish Work Horse Association holds Work Horse days for members. See www.irishworkinghorseassociation.com or call Sandra Schmid on Tel:087-9389867.

BUY MATERIALS

The Irish Work Horse Association is the best place to start making enquiries regarding the purchase of work horses. It has an extensive range of equipment detailed on its website. The organisation also suggests that there is still a fair amount of vintage horse-drawn machinery in Ireland that can be bought quite cheaply and put to work again. In the United States – where the Amish community have always kept working the land with horses – there are a number of companies manufacturing modern horse-drawn ploughs, harrows, manure spreaders etc. Shipping costs are high but Jim Cronin brings in a container full of equipment from the US every year.

BEEKEEPING

What is it?

Beekeeping is the occupation of owning and breeding bees – sometimes for their honey, but often out of sheer fascination with the bees themselves. The honeybee is the most studied and best known of all insects. The Ancient Greeks considered bees to be a mirror image of the ideal society – orderly, industrious and loyal to their leader. The art of beekeeping developed in Ancient Egypt and spread westward to Greece and Rome.

According to legend, Saint Modomnoc from the sixth century AD brought the first bees to Ireland from Wales. The Brehon Laws deal extensively with the right to keep bees, ownership of stray swarms, injuries by bees, stealing bees, etc. Bees were kept in the gardens of the great monasteries of Ireland and honey, beeswax and mead were all very valuable commodities.

Bees were traditionally kept in straw skeps covered in hessian to keep the rain out and sometimes in earthenware pots. Modern-day wooden hives are based on an invention by American clergyman L. L. Langstroth in the late 1800s.

Beekeeping flourished in Ireland in the 1800s and the Irish Beekeepers Association was founded in 1881, continuing its work until 1939. The Federation of Irish Beekeepers Association was founded in 1944 and continues to this day. There has been a great revival of interest in beekeeping in the past decade and in 2005, Ireland hosted over 3,500 beekeepers attending the world conference of beekeepers, Apimondia.

How is it done?

Beekeeping is a hobby best learned from experienced apiarists and for that reason,

the Federation of Irish Beekeepers' Associations suggest that would-be beekeepers attend a one-day introductory course, join their local association and learn the basics of handling bees before investing in a hive and the associated equipment. Aspiring beekeepers should also find out if they are allergic to bee stings and if so, seek medical advice before starting. It is also important to check with neighbours in advance of setting up a hive. As bees don't confine themselves to your property, most suburban gardens are unsuitable for beekeeping.

What do the experts say?

Once you feel comfortable with the basics and have chosen an appropriate site for your hive, then it's time to buy your own small nucleus of bees with a young queen bee. 'It's essential to buy bees from reputable sources to keep disease levels as low as possible,' says Pat Finnegan, who teaches introductory courses in beekeeping. Once put in place, a hive should not be moved more than one metre, unless the new location is more than five kilometres away. Learning how to detect and treat disease – the most prevalent of which is the varroa mite – is a key aspect of beekeeping. It can be a very rewarding pastime, as Finnegan notes: 'you can spend your whole life learning about bees as regard-

less of your knowledge, they will always surprise you.'

How long does it take?

Beekeeping can be a life-long hobby with hands-on periods of activity between April and the end of July each year. The beekeeping year begins in September, when you give the bees stocks of sugary syrup as their winter feed. You then leave them to rest during the winter months. You open the hives in April to check whether the queen is present and laying, and that the colony is free of disease. Then, you check and feed them every eight or nine days as the colony grows, adding extra layers (called supers) to the hive as required. Managing swarming (when the colony attempts to divide into two) is another key skill to learn if you want to have a good crop of honey in September. The honey yield is about twenty kilograms per hive, per year.

Where can I see beekeepers at work?

Attending a beginner course or watching a beekeeping demonstration is the best way to get a taste for beekeeping. Visitors to the Victorian Walled Kitchen Garden at Ashtown Castle in the Phoenix Park can see beehives on the second Saturday of each month (Tel:01 6770095, www.phoenixpark.ie).

SIGN UP

Many local associations in the Federation of Irish Beekeepers run beginner courses over the winter months. The Federation also runs a one-week summer course in the Franciscan College, Gormanston, County Meath. This includes workshops, lectures and demonstations, and attracts beekeepers from home and abroad. See www.irishbeekeeping.ie for full details of all events.

Pat Finnegan holds introductory courses in beekeeping in the The Organic Centre, Rossinver, County Leitrim (theorganiccentre.ie). The Irish Seed Savers Association, Capparoe, Scariff, County Clare also runs a series of seasonally appropriate courses in beekeeping (Tel:061 921866, www.irishseedsavers.ie).

The National Botanic Gardens, Glasnevin, Dublin 9 occasionally hosts talks and demonstrations on beekeeping (Tel:01 8570909), and the Federation of Irish Beekeepers usually have a stand at Bloom, the gardens and food festival held annually in the Phoenix Park; the Dublin Horse Show in the RDS, Ballsbridge, Dublin; and the National Ploughing Championships.

BUY MATERIALS

The Federation of Irish Beekeepers' Association is the best place to seek out information on buying beekeeping equipment and bees. See www.irishbeekeeping.ie for more details.

GREEN WOOD FURNITURE MAKING

What is it?

Green wood furniture is furniture – chairs, small tables and stools – made from recently-cut wood that still contains sap.

The mood and style of green wood furniture has its roots in the simple rustic furniture that was made in Ireland in the eighteenth century. Hedge chairs, in particular, were made by self-styled hedge carpenters. These were woodworkers who used the natural shapes of the branch wood to make components of chairs. These traditional hedge chairs, some of which can be seen in the National Museum of Ireland – Decorative Arts in Dublin, had a large D-shaped slab or plank for the seat, with legs and back spindles tenoned and wedged into the plank. From the eighteenth to the twentieth century, post and rail chairs were made with traditional súgán seating. Súgán (pronounced sue-gawn) is a type of oat straw rope used on farms and produced in the home. It was warm, comfortable, long-lasting, locally avail-able and easily replaced – characteristics that are no longer prioritised in modern production lines. However, the use of hand tools and traditional skills are now valued again in the production of once-off green wood chairs, stools and small tables.

How it is done?

First, you must select the wood. Hazel is generally considered the best, as it sends out very few side shoots as it grows. It is also easy to find in hedgerows and shrubberies. Birch, alder or holly can also be used, as well as maple and hickory, commonly used in the United States. Essentially, any hardwood tree which has been coppiced (the practice of cutting back young trees close to the ground resulting in several new stems growing up) can be used. Most makers choose coppiced wood from locally grown sources.

What's next?

For a green wood chair, you begin by making the back posts from two slightly backward-leaning branches. Then, you make a panel for the back of the chair, joining it to the back posts with mortise and tenon joints. Each panel design is carefully chosen by the chairmaker. Next up are the front frame and sides, followed by the seat and the arms. You can make the seat from planks of wood such as elm, upholster it in leather or felt, or weave it from oat straw rope (as in the traditional súgán chair), rushes or sisal. Although the wood was traditionally pared with a whittling knife, many chairmakers now use more modern tools, such as sanders, cordless drills and a shaving horse.

What do the experts say?

According to Alison Ospina, who gives courses in making green wood furniture at her studio in Skibbereen, it takes about a day to make a small table or stool and about three days to put together a chair, and she insists that the experience will stay with you for life: 'Making these chairs touches a joy in people. I think it's the act of making something beautiful and functional out of a bundle of sticks. Each chair ends up a bit like the person who made it,' she says.

Where can I see green wood furniture?

The best place to see green wood furniture is at the studios of the craftspeople who make them. Currently in Ireland, Alison Ospina (see details below) and Gabriel Casey are the principal makers of this individually-styled type of furniture. The key difference between Ospina's work and Casey's work is that Casey seasons his wood first before making his custom-designed, branch-style chairs. You can see Gabriel Casey's work at his studio, An Geag Cam (The Crooked Branch), Cahermakerla, Lisdoonvarna, County Clare (Tel: 065 7074765, gabriel-casey@eircom.net).

Historic examples of these chairs can be seen at the National Museum of Ireland – Decorative Arts, Collins Barracks, Benburb Street, Dublin 7 and National Museum of Ireland – Country Life, Turlough Park, Castlebar, County Mayo.

SIGN UP

Alison Ospina runs one- and three-day courses in making green wood chairs, small tables and stools from her studio at the Wooden House, Rossnagoose, Skibbereen, County Cork (Tel:028 21890, www.greenwoodchairs.com). The book *Green Wood Chairs: Chairs and Chairmakers of Ireland* by Alison Ospina is available at the course.

BUY MATERIALS

Alison Ospina's *Green Wood Chairs: Chairs and Chairmakers of Ireland* includes an excellent reference section of suppliers of tools and where to source coppiced wood. Coppiced wood from local sources, which is cut and regrows, is the wood of choice for makers of green wood furniture.

WILLOW SCULPTING

What is it?

Willow sculpting is the art of making things from willow. The craft of willow sculpting is closely related to the traditional craft of basket-making. As with basketmaking, willow rods are the material of choice and these are either used in their dried form or shaped into garden furniture (willow shelters, arches, sculptures) as a living form. They are woven into shape by hand, using a range of weaving techniques. The art of weaving structures from willow and hazel dates right back to the Stone Age. Willow was grown in rural Ireland for making all kinds of functional objects for farming and fishing. Each area had its skilled weaver and a small number of farmers grew willow expressly for use in the locality.

Willow sculpting began to flourish again in the 1980s and 1990s. It has become particularly popular in the UK as an environmental outdoor craft. Willow grows quickly and re-generates itself. The cycle of growth, harvesting and more growth provides a sustainable annual supply of rods for new structures. Willow walls, or fedges (i.e. fence-hedges), are also built alongside motorways as an aesthetic buffer against noise and pollution.

How is it done?

Most willow sculptures begin as a sketch or drawing of the proposed piece. Then, you select your material. Many people who work with willow grow several varieties of the tree and choose the wood according to the strength and colour required for an individual piece. Will Wheeler, who gives regular willow-sculpting classes, explains how to build a willow dome. To make a willow dome, you start by preparing the ground, taking out the weeds and putting down a weed membrane. Next, you mark out your circle with white lime and make pilot holes for the rods with a metal bar and mallet; about fifty rods are planted around the circle, each one opposite another, leaving space for an entrance. Then, each standing rod is bent to meet the opposite rod in the middle – the first four rods are the most important to give you the shape of your dome. Then, you plant about one hundred more rods in between the upright ones. These rods are woven together at an angle to give the dome its strength.

What do the experts say?

Living willow sculptures are planted and built on the spot, and can be a great activity for children and adults alike, as Will Wheeler, who gives regular classes, attests: 'Domes make great play areas and shelters for children and also serve as leafy sun shades for adults in the summer time.'

 Making pieces from dried willow is easier. Beth Murphy of Willow Wonder in

Kildare says, 'it helps if you have a grounding in basket-weaving skills, but it's not essential. In my experience, it is much easier to learn how to do willow sculpture than basket-weaving. Willow sculpture is an art form that requires a lot of imagination and creativity; you can make anything from a dome to a dragon.'

Where can I see good examples of willow sculpture?

Murphy and Finch demonstrate their willow sculpting at Electric Picnic, the summer arts and music festival in Stradbally, County Laois. Will Wheeler has built living willow domes at the Greenan Farm and Maze, and the John F. Kennedy Arboretum in New Ross, County Wexford has some fine examples of living willow structures created as observation points to view nature in the park (Tel:051 388171, www.heritageireland.ie).

SIGN UP

Beth Murphy and Paul Finch run Willow Wonder workshops using dried willow and living willow at their cottage in Redhills, County Kildare (Tel:087 6462528, www.willowwonder.net). Will Wheeler teaches adults and school children how to build living willow structures. These include domes, tunnels, fences, arbours and willow garden climbers. The courses include instructions on planting, weaving and maintaining the willow, and are held in Greenan Farm Museums and Maze, Greenan, Rathdrum, County Wicklow (Tel:0404 46000, www.greenanmaze.com).

Terry Dunne (Tel:051 563100, www.terry-theweaver.ie) also teaches living willow structure and sculpture courses in private and community settings in the Wexford area. Introductory courses on willow weaving are also held by the Irish Seed Savers Association, Capparoe, Scariff, Count Clare (Tel:061 921866, www.irishseedsavers.ie).

BUY MATERIALS

The best place to start is to talk to people who already work with willow and see if you can buy dried willow. Alternatively, you could simple buy young willow trees in a garden centre and experiment with them as they begin to grow.

BASKETMAKING

What is it?

Basketry is the art of weaving a basket from strong flexible lengths of willow, hazel or other suitable plants. Basketmaking has been a part of many ancient cultures and in Irish mythology, there are references to wicker currachs. Fishing boats made with wicker bottoms were used until the 1840s along the west coast of Ireland and later in rivers. Wicker was also used to construct houses until the Middle Ages. Willow baskets became very popular in the nineteenth century for use in mills and factories and later for transportation of goods on trains. Dublin, Belfast and many other large towns had basketmaking works at this time, and most rural communities also had at least one basketmaker who made baskets for farm and home use.

Basketmaking fell into decline between the 1950s and 1980s but has since been revived. Many contemporary basketmakers are drawn to the craft because they can be involved in the whole process; from growing and harvesting the willow, to making the basket itself.

Traditionally, baskets were used for carrying and storing turf, fishing for lobsters and straining and serving potatoes. Nowadays, baskets are often used in the home to store vegetables and fuel for the fire. More contemporary-style baskets are experimental art works displayed for their own merit.

What are the most suitable materials?

Willow is the most popular material used nowadays because it is easy to grow and the willow rods have the right balance of strength and flexibility. Once harvested, the willow rods are usually dried for a year, sorted into appropriate lengths and then soaked for up to a week to make them pliable for weaving.

Joe Hogan

Alison Fitzgerald

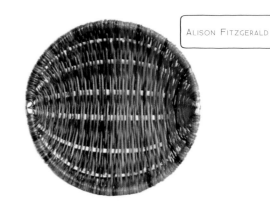

BETH MURPHY

How is it done?

There are two main methods to making a traditional basket. The stake and strand approach involves making a base with a cross in the centre, then weaving willow rods outwards around its arms. Next, you insert upright rods in the base and weave lighter rods around these rods to form the sides of the basket. Finally, you weave rods around the top to create a border. The second type of basket involves making a frame or a hoop, around which you weave the rest of the basket.

What do the experts say?

Frame baskets are 'an easier, less-complicated type to make than the stake and strand,' says Alison Fitzgerald, who gives courses in frame basketmaking. Once you have constructed the circular or oval hoop, you put the ribs of the basket in place. These are the strong elements of the basket, around which the thinner pieces are woven. 'Making a nice hoop is the trickiest part and the secret of the basket. If the hoop is too weak or not well shaped, it will be reflected in your finished basket.'

A professional basketmaker will take about five hours to make a simple log basket The main skills required, according to basketmaker Joe Hogan, are enthusiasm and determination. Strong fingers and hands are a bonus, but undoubtedly they will come with practice.

Where can I see Irish-made baskets?

Many museums have baskets in their collections however, the largest collections of traditional baskets can be seen in the National Museum of Ireland – Country Life, Turlough Park, Castlebar, County Mayo (Tel:094 9031751, www.museum.ie) and the Ulster Folk and Transport Museum, Cultra, Hollywood, County Down (Tel:44 (0)28 90428428, www.nmni.com); there are occasional demonstrations of basketmaking at these museums. The Irish Agricultural Museum at Johnstown Castle Estate, County Wexford has a display of traditional Irish baskets (Tel:053 9184671, www.irishagrimuseum.ie). The Irish Basketmakers Association also has a heritage collection of baskets, which can be borrowed for exhibitions.

SIGN UP

Many professional basketmakers offer courses in their local areas. You can contact them through the secretary of the Irish Basketmakers Association, at www.irishbasketmakers.ie. Alison Fitzgerald gives regular basketmaking courses in the Priory, Benburb, County Tyrone (Tel:44 (0)28 38891486, www.greenwoodbaskets.co.uk). Renate Bradbury gives basketmaking workshops for beginners in Greenan Farm, Rathdrum, County Wicklow (Tel:0404-46000, www.greenanmaze.com), and Beth Murphy and Paul Finch run basketmaking workshops at The Cottage, Redhills, County Kildare (Tel:087 6462528, www.willowwonder.net). Heike Kahle gives courses in Burnafea, Castlewarren, County Kilkenny, and Cathy Hayden gives courses in Tramore, County Waterford (Tel:051 386697).

Basketry is also one of the courses offered at the Organic Centre in Rossinver, County Leitrim (Tel:071 9854338, www.theorganiccentre.ie), the Irish Seed Savers Association, Capparoe, Scariff, County Clare (Tel:061-921866, www.irishseedsavers.ie) and the Centre for Environmental Living and Training in Scariff, County Clare on their Weekend in the Woods (Tel:061 640765, www.celtnet.org).

BUY MATERIALS

It's a good idea to check with local basketmakers who run courses as to how to source the best willow. Getting well-prepared and well-graded willow is crucial. If you can't source it locally, you can buy Irish willow from Barry Noyce in Birr, County Offaly (Tel:086 8241393). Noyce also organises bulk orders of willow from England.

BLACKSMITHING

What is it?

Making objects from metal by heating them in a forge and then hammering them into shape is the essence of blacksmithing. Wrought iron was the metal traditionally used by blacksmiths but this has largely been replaced by a form of low carbon steel called mild steel. Wrought iron and pure iron are still available from specialist providers, and blacksmiths continue to use it in restoration work.

The first recorded workings of iron are with forged meteoroids. Humans have been working with and forging iron for between 2,000 and 6,000 years. Iron replaced bronze as the metal of choice for making weapons during the Bronze and Iron Ages. The blacksmith came to be a central member of society, forging farm implements and weapons as required. During the eighteenth century, the Industrial Revolution made some of the traditional blacksmithing practices obsolete. However, the real demise of the blacksmith came when modern farm machinery replaced work horses on farms. There has been a more recent revival of interest in the craft for design-led work and the modern smith deals mainly with commissioned pieces.

How is it done?

The smith puts the piece of steel into the heart of the coal or gas-fired forge to soften. Then, once it is hot, takes it out and puts it on an anvil and hammers it into shape. The anvil has a flat top and sharp edges for flattening and creating angles, plus a horn at one end which is used to shape the soft steel around if a curved end is required. When the steel cools down slightly, it is returned to the forge to heat up again before further work can be carried out. When the steel heats up, it turns to a bright orange-yellow colour; when it goes back to red, it needs to be heated again. If the steel is allowed to get too hot however, it will start to spark and change to a bright yellow or white colour before melting. The forge itself has side or bottom draughts to keep it at a high temperature.

What do the experts say?

It takes only a few minutes to heat the steel and hammer it into a simple shape. It will take longer to add twists into the design or create more decorative handles. 'The trickiest thing for a beginner is what looks the simplest, for example what's called "drawing out", which is putting a point on a flat or round bar with the hammer. It's all about getting used to the hammering techniques and the fire. The more complex things such as twists and decorations are easier,' says Joe O'Leary, a blacksmith who gives beginners courses with fellow blacksmith, Moss Gaynor (mojometaldesigns.com).

What can be made?

Traditionally, a blacksmith made tradesmen's tools and handheld farm equipment, as well as gates, railings and horse shoes. Nowadays, blacksmiths tend to make decorative pieces, including fireside sets, coat stands, bedsteads, outdoor seats, staircases and indoor and outdoor sculptural pieces. Some blacksmiths still make larger items such as gates and do repair work on old wrought iron gates, railings and staircases.

Where can I see the work of blacksmiths?

Blacksmiths give demonstrations at country fairs from time to time. The Irish Artist Blacksmiths Association website, www.irishblacksmiths.com, is the best place to check for once-off demonstrations. The Irish Agricultural Museum at Johnstown Castle Estate, County Wexford has a replica of a blacksmith's workshop (Tel:053 9184671, www.irishagrimuseum.ie). The National Museum of Ireland – Country Life, Turlough Park, Castlebar, County Mayo also has a display on the traditional craft of blacksmithing (Tel:094 9031755, www.museum.ie).

Joe O'Leary

Donnacha Cahill

177

Calnan and Anhøj

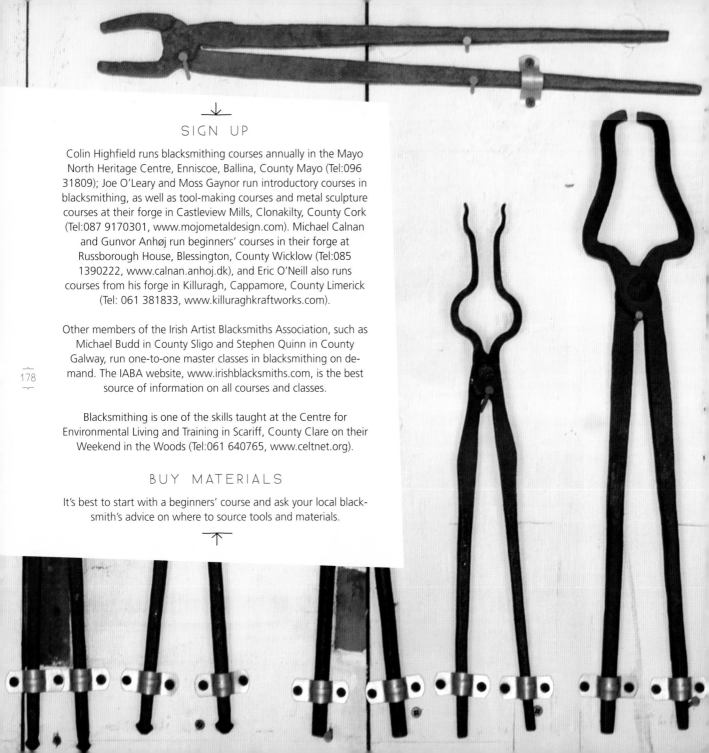

SIGN UP

Colin Highfield runs blacksmithing courses annually in the Mayo North Heritage Centre, Enniscoe, Ballina, County Mayo (Tel:096 31809); Joe O'Leary and Moss Gaynor run introductory courses in blacksmithing, as well as tool-making courses and metal sculpture courses at their forge in Castleview Mills, Clonakilty, County Cork (Tel:087 9170301, www.mojometaldesign.com). Michael Calnan and Gunvor Anhøj run beginners' courses in their forge at Russborough House, Blessington, County Wicklow (Tel:085 1390222, www.calnan.anhoj.dk), and Eric O'Neill also runs courses from his forge in Killuragh, Cappamore, County Limerick (Tel: 061 381833, www.killuraghkraftworks.com).

Other members of the Irish Artist Blacksmiths Association, such as Michael Budd in County Sligo and Stephen Quinn in County Galway, run one-to-one master classes in blacksmithing on demand. The IABA website, www.irishblacksmiths.com, is the best source of information on all courses and classes.

Blacksmithing is one of the skills taught at the Centre for Environmental Living and Training in Scariff, County Clare on their Weekend in the Woods (Tel:061 640765, www.celtnet.org).

BUY MATERIALS

It's best to start with a beginners' course and ask your local black-smith's advice on where to source tools and materials.

CRAFT IN FOCUS:

SEASCAPES

The Knitting and Stitching Show, RDS, Dublin / November 2011
An exhibition of textiles by members of the Crafts Council of Ireland.
The theme for the exhibition was the sea and the underwater world;
its colour, texture, pattern and force. Work took the form of both
literal and abstract interpretation.

Carmel Creaner: Sea Grasses

Anne Kiely: Sea Anemones

Carmel Creaner: Sea Grasses

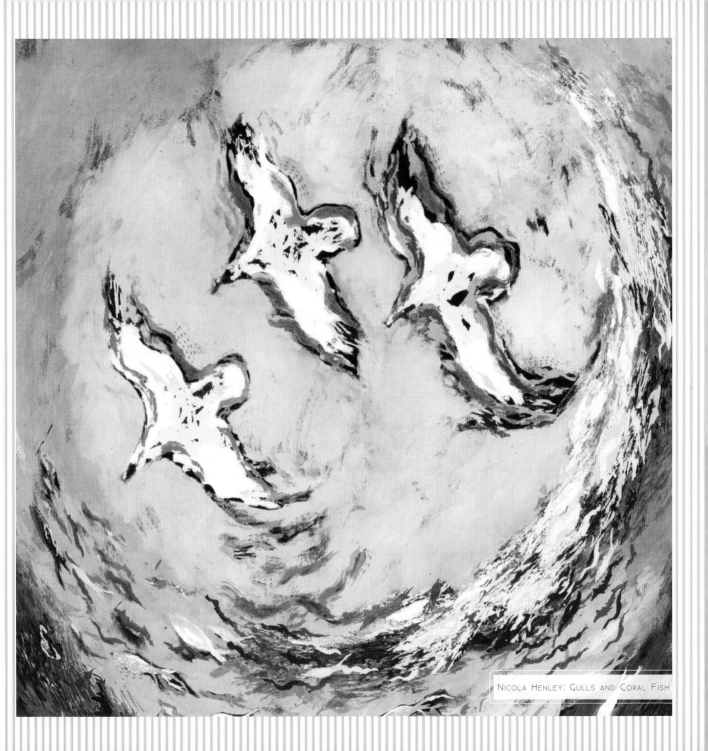

NICOLA HENLEY: GULLS AND CORAL FISH

Ann Duggan: The Postcards

Beth Moran: Into the Deep

Breda McNelis: Oysters and Pearls

Anne Harrington-Rees: Sea Vessel V

NICOLA BROWN: SEA SLUG II

RESTORATION AND CONSERVATION CRAFTS

BOOKBINDING AND BOOK CONSERVATION

What is it?

Bookbinding is the art of putting pages together and encasing them in a hardback cover. This cover or case-binding can be made of a variety of materials such as cloth, leather or printed paper. New books, such as theses, journals and reports for libraries, corporate or academic institutions, are bound to create a special durable finish. Old books, such as Bibles, missals and antiquarian volumes are often rebound as part of their restoration. Special conservation materials and techniques are used when repairing and restoring valuable old books or personal keepsakes.

Ever since books were invented, they were bound. Initially, they were bound with limp materials such as vellum, but from the seventeenth century onwards, books were bound with leather and other more durable materials. In the eighteenth century, the art of bookbinding was at its zenith and Dublin bookbinders were renowned throughout Europe for their technical ability and distinctive designs. Interestingly, the basic equipment used in conservation bookbinding remains unchanged from that used by hand binders of the eighteenth-century Dublin bookbinding era.

What do the experts say?

Bookbinding can be a complicated process, as Barbara Hubert, a bookbinder based in Cork city explains: 'You start by gathering the loose sheets and then you glue or stitch them together. This book block is then forwarded (i.e. made ready for putting on the outside cover), and the back board, front board and spine piece are chosen, cut to size and covered in the required material (e.g. leather, fabric or paper)'. The cover is left to dry overnight. Sometimes, gold lettering is

embossed onto the cover before the book block is glued into it. Then, the bound book is again left to dry overnight.

Conservation bookbinding is a much more specialised craft, as Paul Curtis of Mucros Bookbinding in Muckross House, Killarney, County Kerry acknowledges. 'We save everything from the original book – the cover, boards, leather and even the threads – and we only use acid-free materials in a process that is completely reversible.'

How long does it take?

A bound book can be produced in three days. Although many people expect bookbinding to be a swift process; each piece must go through the proper drying-out process.

Where can I see examples of bookbinding?

Marsh's Library, next to St Patrick's Cathedral is the oldest public library in Ireland. Many of the books in the library are still in their original bindings. It is open on Mondays, Wednesdays,

Thursdays and Fridays from 9:30 AM – 1 PM, and 2 PM – to 5 PM, and on Saturdays from 10 AM – 1 PM. Marsh's Library also houses the Delmas Conservation Bindery and the staff there give public talks on their work from time to time. See www.marshlibrary.ie or Tel:01 4543511 for updates.

The Benjamin Iveagh Library at Farmleigh House in the Phoenix Park has one of the finest collections of Irish bookbinding from the eighteenth, nineteenth and twentieth centuries. The library is visited as part of the guided tours of Farmleigh House, and is also open for use by scholars and readers by prior request to the assistant librarian (Tel:01 8155908, www.farmleigh.ie).

The Long Room in Trinity College Dublin (www.tcd.ie) also has an extensive collection of old bound books but visitors need to request access to the Early Printed Books section to view specific titles. The National University of Ireland universities in Galway, Cork and Dublin also have collections of rare books, which can be viewed on request.

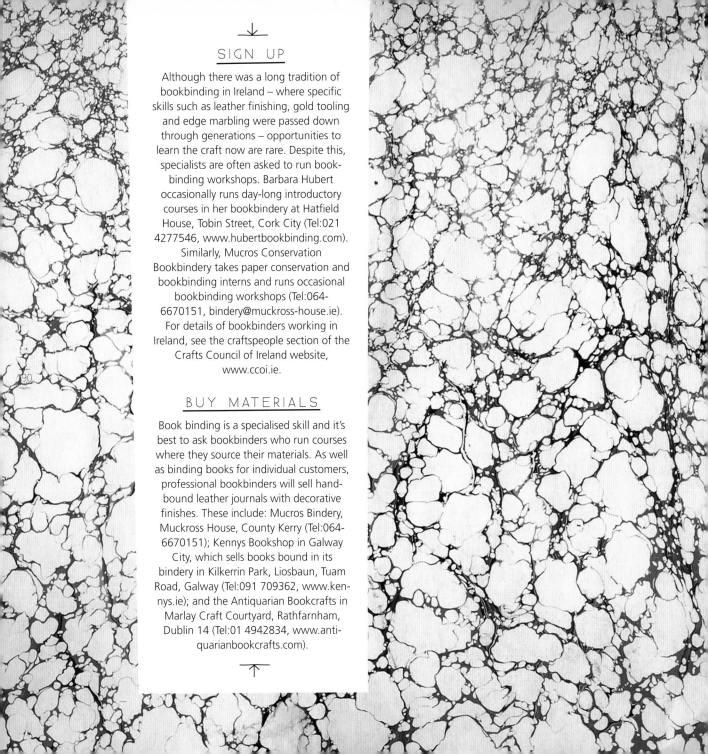

SIGN UP

Although there was a long tradition of bookbinding in Ireland – where specific skills such as leather finishing, gold tooling and edge marbling were passed down through generations – opportunities to learn the craft now are rare. Despite this, specialists are often asked to run bookbinding workshops. Barbara Hubert occasionally runs day-long introductory courses in her bookbindery at Hatfield House, Tobin Street, Cork City (Tel:021 4277546, www.hubertbookbinding.com). Similarly, Mucros Conservation Bookbindery takes paper conservation and bookbinding interns and runs occasional bookbinding workshops (Tel:064-6670151, bindery@muckross-house.ie). For details of bookbinders working in Ireland, see the craftspeople section of the Crafts Council of Ireland website, www.ccoi.ie.

BUY MATERIALS

Book binding is a specialised skill and it's best to ask bookbinders who run courses where they source their materials. As well as binding books for individual customers, professional bookbinders will sell hand-bound leather journals with decorative finishes. These include: Mucros Bindery, Muckross House, County Kerry (Tel:064-6670151); Kennys Bookshop in Galway City, which sells books bound in its bindery in Kilkerrin Park, Liosbaun, Tuam Road, Galway (Tel:091 709362, www.kennys.ie); and the Antiquarian Bookcrafts in Marlay Craft Courtyard, Rathfarnham, Dublin 14 (Tel:01 4942834, www.antiquarianbookcrafts.com).

DECORATIVE PLASTERWORK

What is it?

It's the cornices, friezes and decorative panels you see on walls and ceilings. Most of the historic decorative plasterwork in Ireland dates from the eighteenth and nineteenth centuries. Styles varied from compartmentalised designs in the early eighteenth century, to the more flamboyant Rococo style, featuring figures, trophies, fruit and flowers. This was followed by symmetrical patterns in low relief and the more robust Greek Revival style. Georgian interiors in Dublin have some of the finest examples of stucco work in Europe.

The tradition of applying decorative plasterwork to walls and ceilings of buildings dates back to Ancient Egyptian times. The Romans also used a plaster gypsum to decorate interiors of their houses and public buildings. In Ireland, our medieval cathedrals, abbeys and castles were plastered and sometimes decorated with fresco paintings or relief designs in plasterwork.

Most of the early stucco plasterwork was modelled by hand and this remained the practice until well into the second half of the eighteenth century. However, decorative plasterwork changed in style from the late-seventeenth century right up to the end of the eighteenth century. The bold, compartmentalised designs of the late-seventeenth century and early-eighteenth century were replaced by more figurative style, introduced to Ireland by the Swiss Italian, Bartholomew Cramillion in the 1750s. In his book, *Decorative Dublin*, Peter Pearson describes his work as a masterpiece of composition and modelling; 'his life-size figures, cherubs and swags of fruit are almost free-standing and seem unattached to the ceiling itself,' he writes. By the mid-eighteenth

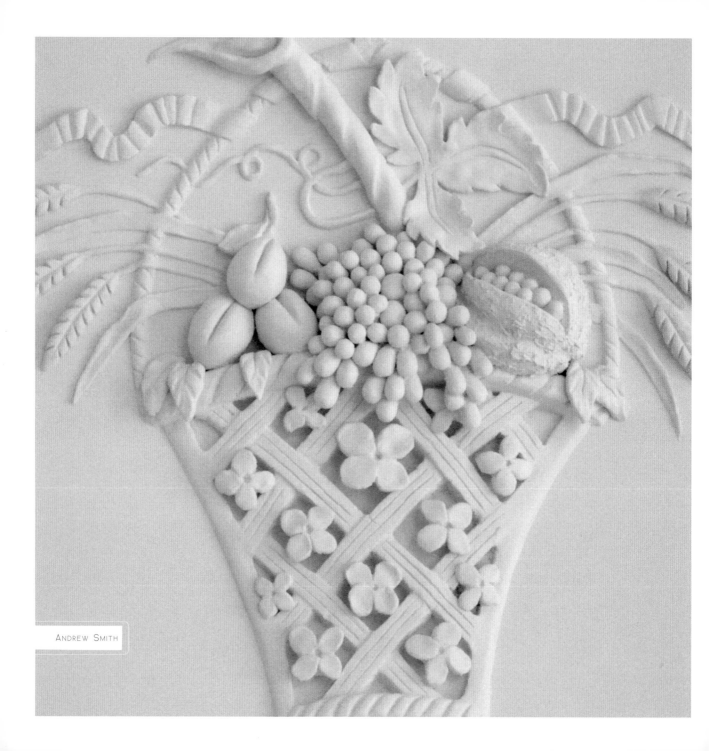

century, much of the plasterwork was gilded. Some ceilings were also brightly painted with a palette of oranges, blues, reds, greens and golds, inspired by the brightly-tinted wall paintings which were then being excavated in places like Pompeii and Herculaneum in Italy. After the Rococo style, low-relief geometric patterns became the dominant design in the late Georgian period.

The craft of the decorative plasterers (or stuccodores) fell into two main categories – freehand and cast. Once-off pieces were generally hand modelled in situ – sometimes on a scaffold under a ceiling while repeated ornaments such as rosettas were cast on a bench in a room below. Stuccodores kept a store of models or casts to re-use for other jobs and often worked away in their studios during the winter months when they couldn't plaster – due to the risk of frost damage to the plasterwork.

Rococo-style ornaments were generally reinforced with a thin piece of oak or a nail and then pushed in the setting plaster. Larger pieces were reinforced with pieces of wire and canvas before being fixed to the ceiling or cornice. From the 1760s onwards, most decorative plasterwork was made up of cast elements. As fresh plaster sets quickly, the stuccodore sometimes mixed it with glue, sour milk or even beer to delay the process to give him more time to model.

How is it restored?

First you have to work out which materials were used originally. The papier mâché that was used in some cases would disintegrate completely if you used plasterwork restoration techniques. The layers of paint must also be expertly analysed before restoration begins. Overpainting, which obscures the detail of the plasterwork, is one of the most common problems, and it is essential that solvent-based paint removers are used. Once the layers of paint are removed, you will be able to spot any defects.

What do the experts say?

You must first trace the plasterwork to pinpoint the exact location of missing elements, before modelling replacements by hand and adding them to the original plasterwork. 'I model a core coat, which is a bit coarser, and leave it to dry for a few days, or a week,' explains Andrew Smith, an expert who restores and creates original decorative plasterwork. 'Then, I finish it off with a smooth coat of lime and plaster. Two coats of distemper paint are added at the end.' If the damaged area is a repeated geometrical pattern, you will be able to use a mould instead.

How long does it take?

Removing the layers of paint from the plasterwork is often the most time-consuming element of the work. The time needed to restore the plasterwork itself depends on the extent of damage. Drying time between core and final coats and repainting must also be factored in, so that creating a new decorative plasterwork ceiling can take up to six months.

Where can I see fine examples of decorative plasterwork?

The quality and quantity of decorative plasterwork in Dublin is unrivalled by any other European city, according to art historian Peter Pearson. Decorative plasterwork was a feature even in some modest Georgian houses, although much of this hasn't survived. Public buildings with significant decorative plasterwork ceilings include the restored chapel at the Royal Hospital, Kilmainham, Dublin; Parliament House (now the Bank of Ireland on College Green); the Chapel and Exam Hall of Trinity College Dublin (on guided tour); City Hall and Dublin Castle (on guided tour) are good for starters. Other examples can be seen at Russborough House, Blessington, County Wicklow (Tel:045 865239 www.russborough.ie); Castletown House, Celbridge, County Kildare (Tel: 01 6288252) and Fota House, Fota Island, County Cork (Tel:021 4815543, www.fotahouse.com). Many country houses open to visitors throughout Ireland also have fine examples of decorative plasterwork; see www.heritageireland.ie for a list of properties managed by the Office of Public Works.

SIGN UP

Dublin Civic Trust run occasional seminars in historic decorative plasterwork finishes (Tel:01 4756911, www.dublin-civictrust.ie). The Irish Georgian Society strongly recommends expert advice is sought before decorative plasterwork is repaired or restored. Andrew Smith gives public talks on the dos and don'ts of restoring decorative plasterwork at the Irish Georgian Society Traditional Building and Conservation Skills in Action exhibition (Tel:01 6767053, www.igs.ie). The Irish Georgian Society also holds a register of skilled craftspeople who conserve and restore decorative plasterwork.

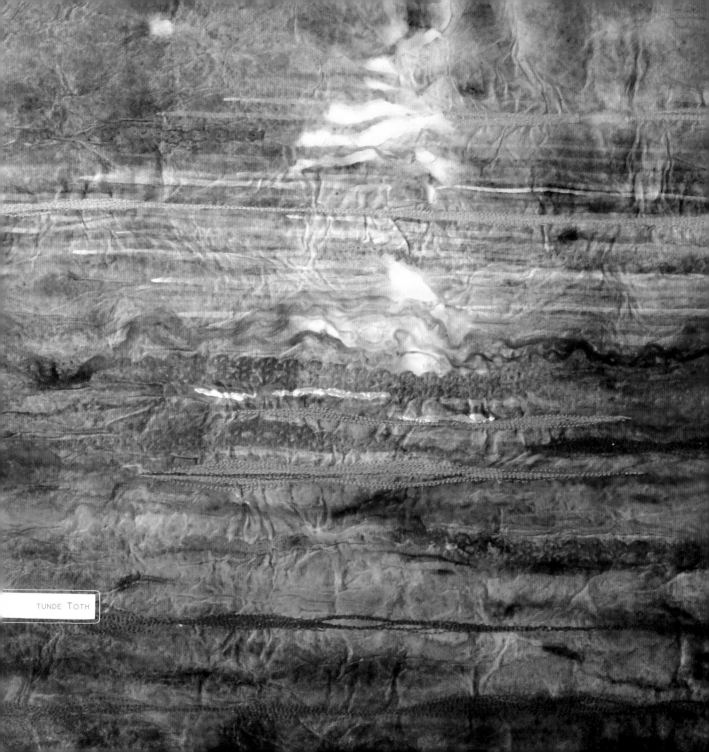

TUNDE TOTH

PAPER MAKING

How was paper first made?

The Chinese are first credited with the invention of paper. In the year 104 AD, Chinese scribe, Ts'ai Lun made a thin, felted material which was formed from moistened vegetable fibres placed on flat porous moulds. Prior to this, woven fabric was used as a precursor to paper. But developments in calligraphy – new brushes and fluid pigment – created a demand for a new cheaper substance to write on.

The type of early paper varied across countries, depending on the climate, the types of available plant fibres, and cultural and aesthetic preferences. Paper making developed in China, Japan and Korea several centuries before it was made in Europe. From China, paper making spread across Asia to the Middle East but it remains a relatively rare craft in Europe until the development of the printing press enlarged its market.

In Europe, paper was traditionally made from cotton and linen rags which were beaten up to form a pulp. The rags were pounded in water by large wooden stampers connected to a water wheel. The pulp was then placed into a large vat of water, into which the papermakers frames were dipped. The frames were like large picture frames with wire mesh across it. The paper maker dipped the frame into the vat, catching a layer of pulped rags onto the mesh. When this settled on the woven structure, it was carefully transferred onto felts and allowed to dry. Paper made in this way had the consistency of blotting paper and needed to be sized (dipped into a basin of glue or gelatine) before it could be written or drawn on.

Different meshes created different patterns on the paper. The earliest paper maker's frame had a mould mesh which created distinctive vertical and horizontal lines visible in paper when you held it up to the light. The paper made from this mesh was called laid paper. Later – around 1755 – another type of mould was developed which had a tightly woven wire in the mesh. This type of paper was called wove paper.

Each paper mill had its own distinctive water mark. Sometimes a watermark was used to date a piece of paper. At other times, it simply marked out the region or place it was made.

Wood pulp began to replace rags as a raw material for making paper from the early 1800s onwards. However, paper made from wood pulp wasn't as strong or durable as paper made from rags. It also discolours and becomes brittle over time. Repairing such paper is the work of paper conservators.

How do you make paper nowadays?

You start by mixing chips or shavings of wood or other fibrous materials with water. You can also add petals, dried flowers, seeds, grass, spices, herbs, newspaper or parts of photographs for decoration. Then, you slide a mesh or mould into the liquid pulp. The materials form a thin layer on the deckle – the top of the mesh – which you then rock back and forth in the water to get an even covering. You can create a watermark by stitching patterns or letters on to the mesh. Next, having allowed as much of the water as possible to drain from the moist pulp, you use a sheet of felt to absorb the remaining liquid from what will become your sheet of paper. You put this in a press to dry overnight.

What's next?

The next day, you can paint the paper with a special paste to strengthen it for writing

on. Then, you can marble it by putting it back in a mixture of water and ink. You can make pasted paper by mixing colour with paste and applying it to paper using techniques such as combing, strippling, or freestyle drawing. Then you rinse, dry or press your marbled or pasted paper.

How long does it take?

It takes a matter of minutes to make a sheet of paper but you'll need to allow a day or two for it to dry out fully and be ready for use.

What about paper conservation?

Paper conservation is the treatment and re-pair of damaged paper. It is a much slower process as it involves meticulous removal of water marks, brown spots (known as fox-ing) or other stains with vulcanized rubber. You fix tears by adding strips of fine Japanese paper to the back of the paper before retouching its front.

Where can I see examples of handmade paper?

Apart from making it or buying it (see below), the most likely place you'll see handmade paper is on specially designed invitations to christenings, weddings or other celebrations. Daintree Paper Shop, 61 Camden Street, Dublin 2 (Tel:(01)475 7500, www.daintree.ie) stocks a great range of handmade paper and card.

SIGN UP

Paper conserver Pat McBride gives two-day workshops in paper making by hand in the Paper Conservation Studio, The Design Tower, Grand Canal Quay, Dublin 2 (Tel:086-2451318, thedesigntower.blogspot.com). Hungarian-born paper maker and founder of the Irish Paper Art Network, Tunde Toth gives work-shops in traditional and contemporary papermaking and silk fibre paper making in art galleries, museums, studios and schools (paperartnetwork@gmail.com, tundetune@gmail.com).

BUY MATERIALS

Most arts and craft shops stock some different types of handmade paper, pastes and paper dyes. Particularly good shops for supplies are: O'Sullivan Graphic Supplies, 14/15 Camden Street, Dublin 2 (Tel:01 4789460, www.osulli-vangraphics.com); M Kennedy & Sons, 12 Harcourt Street, Dublin 2, (Tel:01 4751749); and Cork Art Supplies, 26-28 Princes Street, Cork City (Tel:021 4277488, www.corkartsup-plies.com).

STUART McGRATH

STONE CARVING AND CONSERVATION

What is it?

Carving stone is a key part of sculpting stone, but cutting letters out of stone for headstones or other commemorative pieces is a traditional skill that is still practised today. The conservation of stone involves the repair or replacement of damaged stone on older buildings.

Stone is the most durable building material known and has been used throughout the centuries for construction and decoration. Because it is hard to cut and heavy to move, it is an expensive material and used principally for important buildings such as churches, banks or other public buildings.

In the eighteenth and nineteenth centuries, stone buildings were highly ornamented with carved features and decorative details. Stone ornamentation is most usually found in the classical or Gothic traditions. The classical tradition was used for entrances and gateways, for example the portico at the General Post Office on O'Connell Street, or the many doorcases on Georgian houses. Decorative features such as cupolas, fountains and mantelpieces were also made of stone. 'Carved capitols, sculpted heads and urns are all part of this ancient architectural tradition, the origins of which can be traced back to Greek and Roman sources,' writes Peter Pearson in his chapter on stone in *Decorative Dublin*.

Granite, limestone and sandstone were the principal types of stone available in Ireland. There was also some slate and marble. Softer stones, such as Portland and Caen stone were imported.

The stonemason's craft ranged from carving large coats of arms and friezes, to humble name plaques. During the

nineteenth century, more eclectic styles of architecture became fashionable and with that more flamboyant decorative stone carving with features from Egyptian temples, French Gothic cathedrals, English Tudor mansion and Flemish Renaissance town houses and even Celtic traditions, according to Peter Pearson. The tradition of stone carving has not disappeared, although the detail is often much less complex and some would say, less interesting as a result.

How is it done?

Traditionally, stone is carved with a mallet and chisel. Restoration stone-carving is when pieces of stone are grafted onto older stone which has been chipped or damaged. The conservationist approach to caring for old stone buildings avoids replacement of stone where possible, and always recommends the use of lime mortar if re-pointing is required. Rusted ties or cramps used in the construction of stone walls may also need to be replaced with stainless steel or phosphor bronze fixings.

How long does it take?

It takes about fifteen minutes to carve each letter on a stone. However, the time required to repair damaged stone in old buildings depends entirely on the extent of damage and whether re-pointing and the insertion of new ties and cramps is required.

Where can I see examples of stone masonry and carving?

You can see plenty of fine examples of stone carving and historic stone sculpting at both Mount Jerome and Glasnevin cemeteries in Dublin. Dublin's City Hall in Dame Street has superbly restored stone work on the exterior and interior walls. The Museum Building in Trinity College Dublin has some incredible examples of Irish marble. Christ Church Cathedral has one of the oldest examples of stonework in the Romanesque door of the South transept. The Gandon-built Custom House is one of the finest examples of a classical stone structure in Ireland. And, of course, stone bridges over rivers and canals across the country are fine local examples of stonework.

SIGN UP

Sculptor, stone carver and stone
conserver, Philip Quinn runs community
workshops in stone-carving. He demonstrates stone letter cutting and stone
carving, and offers people a chance to
try it out at the Irish Georgian Society
Traditional Building Skills in Action
exhibitions, as well as giving workshops
at other County Fairs and Festivals. See
www.stonemad.ie or Tel:086 2532474
for full details of his workshops
and demonstrations.

Stonemason Pat McAfee also gives
occasional public lectures on masonry
structures and conservation. The Building
Limes Forum Ireland actively promotes
the use of lime mortar (www.build-
inglimesforumireland.com). Stone
masons and stone carvers who follow
conservation methods can be found on
the Irish Georgian Society's Register of
Traditional Building Skills (www.igs.ie).

↑

205

PHILIP QUINN

CALLIGRAPHY

What is it?

Calligraphy is the art of decorative writing, which dates back to the Roman Empire in this part of the world. At that time, the Roman alphabet – adapted from the Greek alphabet – became the system of written communication common to all the languages of the Western world. The classical form of Roman lettering still survives on stone carved monumental inscriptions.

Throughout the Roman Empire, reed brushes or pens, and later quill pens were used to write on papyrus, parchment and vellum for important documents and manuscripts. Less formal documents were inscribed on wax tablets, which could be re-used by warming the wax to smooth the surface. As the influence of Rome declined, new writing evolved in the Christian scholarship of Europe. One of the finest examples of such work can be seen in the eighth-century Book of Kells in Trinity College Dublin. Script writing was revised and refined over the following centuries, giving rise to styles such as Carolingian (named after Charlemagne, King of Franks) and later Gothic.

The invention of printing in the late-fifteenth century signalled the end of the long-established tradition of writing by scribes and scholars. However, the formal scripts of the Gothic and Renaissance periods were used as the models for the newly created printers types. The calligrapher's skills were still used for manuscripts and documents not intended for widespread distribution. Samples of different scripts were also reproduced by the technique of engraving on copper for printing. With improved methods of printing, the nineteenth century became a barren period for calligraphers. However, the twentieth century brought about a revival of interest in the historical developments, traditional tools and materials used for calligraphy. Some calligraphers also became the designers of widely used typefaces.

Nowadays, calligraphy is used both commercially and artistically in the creation of presentation scrolls, wedding stationery, certificates, handmade books and other personalised pieces of work.
Calligraphers draw on a huge range of ancient and modern alphabets, which include Roman, Uncial, Insular, Carolingian, Gothic, Italic and Copperplate.
Contemporary calligraphers also improvise and use hybrid scripts.

How it is done?

Calligraphers usually work on a sloped surface using a chisel-edged nib, or for certain alphabet styles such as copperplate, a flexible pointed nib.
Contemporary calligraphers often use other writing tools – homemade pens, reed pens and brushes. For example, the Irish calligrapher Denis Brown writes on glass with a dentist's drill (www.quill-skill.com). Ink, gouache and watercolours are used on a variety of fine papers, vellum or other materials. These are sometimes prepared with watercolour washes, layers of colour, dyes or pastels. The personal style of a highly-skilled calligrapher is identifiable to those who view and collect contemporary works by calligraphers.

What do the experts say?

The length of time devoted by calligraphers to each new piece depends entirely on the style of work and pace of the individual artist. Beginners start with a basic script derived from the ninth century Carolingian period and use Roman capital letters. The family characteristics of an alphabet have to be mastered first, paying attention to the weight and slant of the letters, the pen angle and other distinguishing features. 'An artistic sensibility combined with a sense of form and design and a fascination with the tradition itself is what makes a good calligrapher. The expressive potential of writing to amplify a text is what attracts people to calligraphy,' says Kevin Honan, an Irish calligrapher who also makes books.

Where can I see examples of calligraphy?

The Books of Kells in Trinity College Dublin (www.tcd.ie) is a fine example of calligraphy. The Chester Beatty Library, Dublin Castle also has an extensive range of Western, Islamic and Japanese/Chinese calligraphy – particularly from religious manuscripts (Tel:01 4070750, www.cbl.ie). The Bank on College Green, Dublin 2 is a pub famous for having a facsimile of The Book of Kells on display.

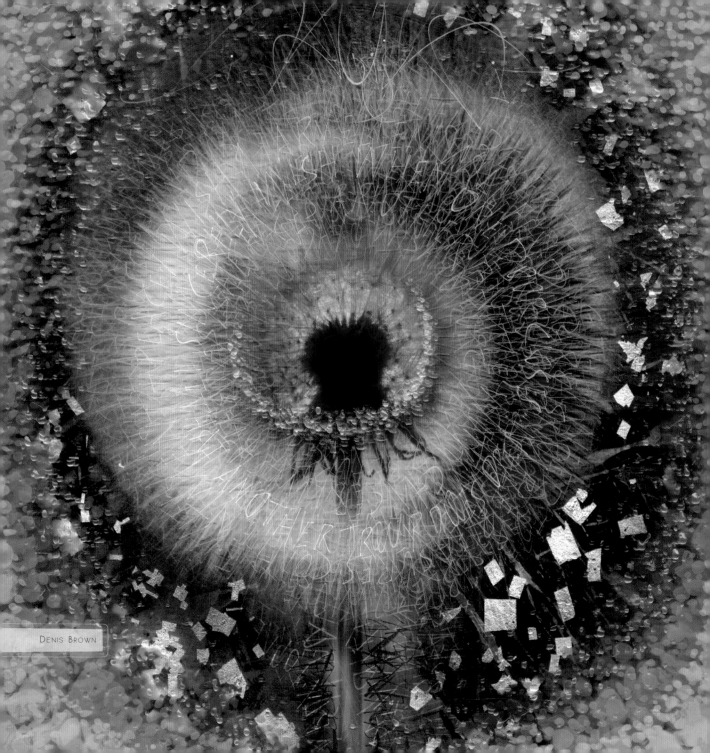

DENIS BROWN

SIGN UP

The Association of Irish Calligraphers, or Peannairí (www.calligraphy.ie) holds classes, workshops and demonstrations in various venues throughout the year. There are also open meetings on the last Thursday of each month (excluding July/August) in the Oatlands College, Stillorgan, County Dublin, and new members are always welcome.

Peannairí also works with schools and colleges to preserve and continue the tradition of calligraphy and to encourage the exploration of contemporary letter art. Members of the association tutor students to Diploma level through Peannairí's affiliation with the Calligraphy and Lettering Arts Society (Tel:087-2560762, info@calligraphy.ie). The National Print Museum, Beggar's Bush Barracks, Haddington Road, Dublin 4 has occasional exhibitions on calligraphy and also runs workshops for adults and children (Tel:01 6603770, www.nationalprintmuseum.ie).

BUY MATERIALS

Most good art and craft shops have starter kits for calligraphy, which include plenty of examples of different fonts to work on. Particularly good shops for supplies are: O'Sullivan Graphic Supplies, 14/15 Camden Street, Dublin 2 (Tel:01 4789460, www.osullivangraphics.com); M Kennedy & Sons, 12 Harcourt Street, Dublin 2 (Tel:01 4751749); and Cork Art Supplies, 26-28 Princes Street, Cork City (Tel:021 4277488, www.corkartsupplies.com). A great shop for pens and nibs is the Pen Corner, College Green, Dublin 2 (Tel:01 6793641).

DENIS BROWN

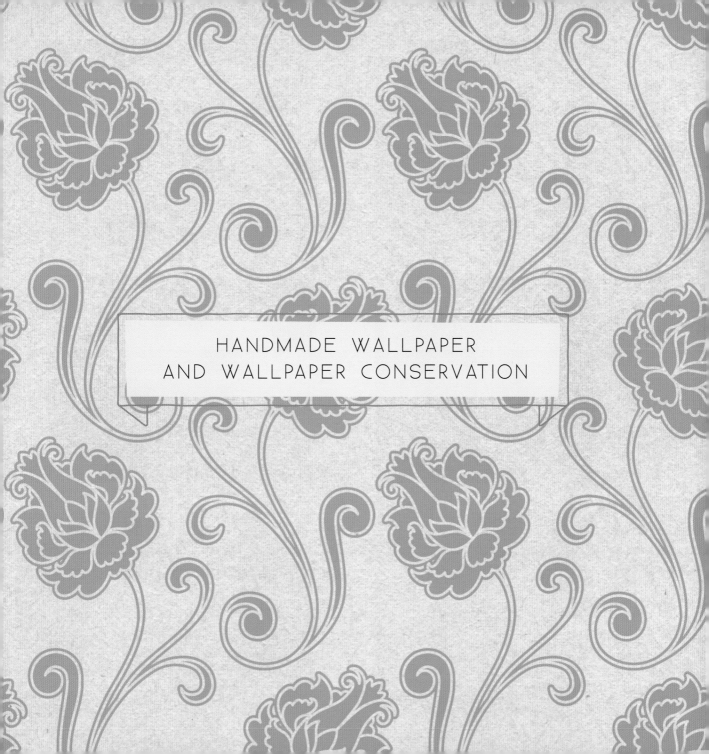

HANDMADE WALLPAPER
AND WALLPAPER CONSERVATION

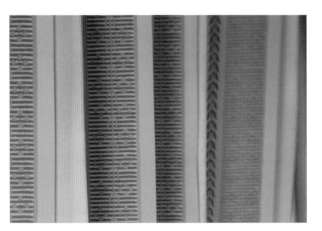

DAVID SKINNER STUDIO

What is it?

You can make wallpaper using block or screen-printing techniques. Conserving wallpaper involves using a range of techniques to restore old and usually valuable wallpaper.

The oldest known example of wallpaper in Ireland is a small piece that was found on the back of a door at the Royal Hospital Kilmainham. Painted and over-printed with a flock design made from finely chopped wool fibres, it was made at the end of the seventeenth century.

The fashion for decorating rooms with wallpaper had developed widely by the mid-eighteenth century. Most wallpapers were handprinted in lengths of about six or nine feet (1.8 metres or 2.7 metres). Wallpapers also came in 10 metre/12 yard rolls from very early on. Some of the earliest wallpapers were imported from China, an example of which can be seen in Carton House, Maynooth, County Kildare.

In the eighteenth and nineteenth centuries, wallpaper was made and hung by tradesmen known as paper stainers. Patterns varied from nature themes (plants, foliage, flower and birds) to more classical motifs (swags of fruit, garlands and arabesques). Flock wallpaper and plain-coloured wallpaper were also popular.

The Victorian period heralded a great change in wallpaper production as paper became more widely available on rolls and the printing process mechanised. Designs were mass-produced and wallpaper became affordable for everyone.

Kildare Wallpapers was established in 1938 with a factory in Newbridge. They made wallpaper there until it closed in 1975. Wallpaper was also manufactured in Bray, County Wicklow by Coxons. Many of these wallpapers can still be found at the back of cupboards and in attics in people's homes.

Although the use of wallpaper fell into decline towards the end of the last century, wallpaper has become fashionable again for use on a feature wall or panel, rather than throughout a room.

How is it done?

Once you have chosen your pattern, you print a colour at a time using screens (which work like stencils) or wooden blocks (on which the pattern is carved). 'You build up the design adding each subsequent colour,' explains David Skinner, who specialises in recreating Irish wallpaper patterns from the Georgian and Victorian era. These patterns are reproductions of wallpaper patterns found in Great Irish Houses such as Strokestown House, County Roscommon, Birr Castle, County Offaly and Fota House in County Cork.

What about conservation?

This can involve surface cleaning, re-attaching peeling paper, stabilising flaking pigment, repairing tears or re-lining fragile paper. Usually problems with the wall – particularly to do with damp – have to be addressed as part of the process. Projects can take from a day to several weeks or even months, depending on the specifics of the situation. 'No two projects are ever alike. Some papers, particularly nineteenth-century ones, can be made from poor quality paper, which is very fragile. Earlier eighteenth-century papers tend to be easier to handle, being made from high-quality rag paper,' says Skinner.

What do the experts say?

Printing wallpaper can be labour intensive and you might spend a whole day on one colour. 'We use water-based inks, which take two to three hours to dry before you can start the next colour,' says David Skinner. The time you'll need to conserve historic wallpaper depends entirely on its condition. Sometimes, you can clean and repair in situ; at other times, you have to remove it – perhaps during building works – and replace it once you have restored it. 'It's always better to preserve what's there rather than replace it with a modern copy, however good that is,' says Skinner, who suggests that even wallpaper from the 1930s to the 1950s now have historic value.

Where can I see historic wallpaper patterns?

Historic wallpapers haven't survived in the same quantity as decorative plasterwork. However, there are a number of fine examples still to be seen in historic homes throughout Ireland. These include: Fota House, Fota Island, County Cork (Tel 021 4815543, www.fotahouse.com); Strokestown House, County Roscommon (Tel:071 9633013, www.strokestownpark.ie); Belvedere House, Mullingar, County Westmeath (Tel:044 9349060, www.belvederehouse.ie); the Swiss Cottage, Kilcommon, Cahir, County Tipperary (Tel:052 7441144); Newbridge House, Donabate, County Dublin (Tel:01 8436534, www.newbridgehouseandfarm.com) and Malahide Castle, Malahide, County Dublin (Tel:01 8462184, www.malahidecastle.com).

David Skinner has also produced a wallpaper pattern book of the Great Houses of Ireland collection, which is available online at www.skinnerwallpaper.com. David Skinner also has an archive of historic Irish wallpaper patterns and is interested in seeing samples of historic wallpaper patterns that people discover in their homes.

DAVID SKINNER: COOLATTIN

SIGN UP

David Skinner and his business partner, Hal Clements are experts in wallpaper conservation and historic handprinted wallpaper in Ireland. There aren't any workshops or training courses in making or conserving wallpaper in Ireland. However, David Skinner gives occasional public lectures on the history and conservation of Historic Irish Wallpapers during the Irish Georgian Society's Traditional Building and Conservation Skills in Action exhibition. See www.igs.ie or Tel: 01 676 7053 for details.

MAKING AND RESTORING DECORATIVE FANLIGHTS

What is it?

Restoring a fanlight – the small window over a door – involves replacing any cracked glass with mouth blown cylinder glass to match the original, and using glazing bars and lead moldings to re-place broken or missing parts of the metal profile of the fanlight and other decorative features.

Dublin fanlights from the Georgian, Victorian and Edwardian eras are often more detailed and elaborately decorated than those in London, Edinburgh, Bristol

ALAN TOMLIN

or Bath, and people are now more aware of their particular beauty and historic significance.

Fanlights were originally put in place to bring light into an otherwise dark hallway. Sidelights at either side of the door served the same function. The doorcase and fanlight formed the focal point of interest on the house frontage and still do to this day.

The first fanlights were made of solid timber with glazing bars radiating out from a central point. These wooden fanlights date from 1710-1760 and were common in the plain arched doorways of the houses of that period. Although mainly found in houses, fanlights were

also used in some public buildings, for example the Custom House in Dublin.

In the latter half of the eighteenth century, timber fanlights became more delicate, resulting in the refined spider's web effect made up of the thinnest strips of wood, writes Peter Pearson in his book, *Decorative Dublin*. Ornaments, such as rosettes and urns, were made from gesso or putty and glued to the timber's glazing bars.

From the 1770s onwards, fanlights were constructed in metal and faced with lead ornamentation. This metal structure was fastened to a semi-circular wooden frame, which was fitted to the brick arch of the doorway. Fanlights were generally painted in an off-white or stone colour. Although semi-circular fan-lights are the best-known, rectangular or oval shapes were also popular in some towns and cities around Ireland. Fanlights were used in the grandest mansions to the humblest farmhouses, gate lodges and cottages. Some of them were designed with oil lanterns incorporated so that the hallway and doorstep were lit by day and by night.

Until the 1830s, clear, hand-blown glass was used in fanlights, but from then onwards, coloured glass became popular and by the mid-nineteenth century, acid-etched glass and colour panes were the norm in fanlights, which by then were also used in internal hallways, on staircases and landings. Fanlights remain one of the most attractive features of houses from the Georgian, Victorian and Edwardian periods and the skills required for their conservation deserve to be appreciated and celebrated.

How is it done?

Firstly, you outline the pattern on the new glass with a stained glass pigment and fire this in a kiln. Then, you add each different-coloured detail and shading of the pattern one at a time, putting it in the kiln after each colour is added. The firing fuses each part of the pattern into the glass,'

What do the experts say?

'It's important to match the design of the glasswork to the period of the house, and this can sometimes require research into other nearby houses where the stained glass hasn't been damaged,' explains Alan Tomlin who restores and makes fanlights, sidelights and other stained-glass windows in period houses, churches and other public buildings (Tel:01 2956167, info@irishstainedglass.com). He also makes new fanlights, which can include stained glass with detail, coloured glass or plain glass fitted into a decorative or simple frame, depending on the client's taste. It generally takes about two weeks to repair or design and make a fanlight.

SIGN UP

The apprenticeship approach to learning traditional crafts died out in the 1960s and 1970s. Opportunities to learn or learn about such skills as fanlight restoration now depend entirely on whether the few remaining practitioners decide to give workshops or seminars. Currently, there aren't any courses available but Alan Tomlin from www.irishstainedglass.com sometimes shows examples of his work at the annual Irish Georgian Society's Traditional Building and Conservation Skills in Action exhibition at Farmleigh, Phoenix Park. See www.igs.ie or Tel:01 6767053 for full details. The Dublin Civic Trust (www.dublincivictrust.ie) is also a good place to seek out expert advice.

FURNITURE RESTORATION

What is it?

Furniture restoration involves the repair of upholstered chairs, antique tables and other furniture using conservation approaches in cabinet-making, upholstery, gilding and French polishing.

The furniture that requires restoration generally originated in the seventeenth, eighteenth and nineteenth centuries. Irish furniture from the seventeenth century was mainly made from oak, although from the 1660s onwards, furniture made from walnut also became fashionable. French and Dutch refugees fleeing wars in Europe brought continental styles and techniques and new types of furniture such as chests were introduced to Ireland. Carving, veneers and inlays in pearl and ivory with contrasting wood became popular. Beds were the most valued pieces of furniture in Irish houses during the seventeenth century and large four poster beds were embellished with luxurious decorative curtains.

In the eighteenth century, mahogany from the West Indies became the wood of choice although walnut was still in style. Due to increased trade with the Far East, Chinese decorative work, Japanese lacquer and Japanese furniture became popular. From the mid-eighteenth century, satinwood and other veneers were introduced and the style of this Georgian period was defined by the great cabinet makers, such as Chippendale, Shearer, Hepplewhite and Gillows.

Regency furniture dominated the early part of the nineteenth century. Mahogany continued to be popular and there was a great revival of interest in classical design. The Victorian style of furniture drew influences from French eighteenth and early-nineteenth century designs.

L'Art Nouveau and the Arts and Crafts movement began in the 1890s and architects like Mackintosh and Voysey strongly influenced furniture styles in England. Imitations and variations of antique styles were popular in Edwardian furniture of the early twentieth-century, but after World War II, modular furniture came into vogue alongside imitations recalling Chippendale.

How is it done?

To restore an upholstered chair or couch, the cover is removed and the piece is stripped back to its bare frame. Cabinet makers will then repair or replace mortise and tenon joints, as well as missing pieces of timber, which will be shaped or carved to match the original frame. Loose legs and arms are also repaired and the piece is thoroughly checked and treated for woodworm if necessary. A gilder will then strip any areas of the gilding where plasterwork is damaged or artificial gold paint has been added. Ten to fifteen coats of gesso is then applied to help solidify any loose plasterwork. After a fine sanding, sheets of gold leaf are then put in place and burnished using a gilder's knife. The upholstery is repaired, layer by layer.

What's next?

A herring bone webbing is then tacked into the base of the seat. The coil springs are sewn into place by hand and inter-laced with sisal cord;. afterwards a

hessian fabric is tacked on. The old horse hair which has been washed, dried and hand-teased is put on top of this. Another layer of hessian is tacked in place, then a layer of wadding, a lining and finally the cover itself.

The covers can be traditional patterns, such as Gainsborough, or made from silk or damask. The gimp (border) is glued on at the end, and the piece of furniture is lightly sanded between coats of wood stain, which can be applied up to 100 times during the French-polishing process.

How long does it take?

Each stage requires varying lengths of time for glues and layers of gesso or polish to dry. It takes up to two weeks for an upholstered chair to be fully restored and about ten days for a large table to be French polished.

Where can I see examples of fine Irish furniture?

Ireland has a rich and varied collection of period furniture, ranging from Baroque sideboards to tea and games tables, bookcases and mirrors.

Irish Furniture by The Knight of Glin (the late Desmond Fitzgerald) and James Peill is the best record available of historic Irish furniture. It includes a directory of furniture in public and private buildings throughout Ireland. From it, you can select country houses, churches and public buildings to go to look at furniture from the different architectural periods. These will include anything from medieval choir stalls to magnificent drawing room suites made for the Great Houses of the eighteenth century. The book also includes an index of Irish furniture makers and craftsmen from the eighteenth century, a time when Dublin was a centre for luxury crafts – fine silverware, furniture, ceramics, glass, textiles and bookbinding.

Suggested place to see such craftsmanship include Russborough House, Blessington, County Wicklow (Tel:045 865239, www.russborough.ie); Castletown House, Celbridge, County Kildare (Tel:01 6288252; Kilkenny Castle, Kilkenny, (Tel:056 7704100, www.kilkennycastle.ie); the Royal Hospital, Kilmainham (Tel:01 6129900).

The National Museum Ireland – Decorative Arts at Collins Barracks, Dublin has also recently opened furniture galleries, featuring furniture dating from the seventeenth to the twentieth century (Tel:01 6777444, www.museum.ie). Bunratty Castle, County Clare also has a fine collection of medieval furniture (www.bunrattycollection.com). See www.heritageireland.ie for other country houses with furniture collections.

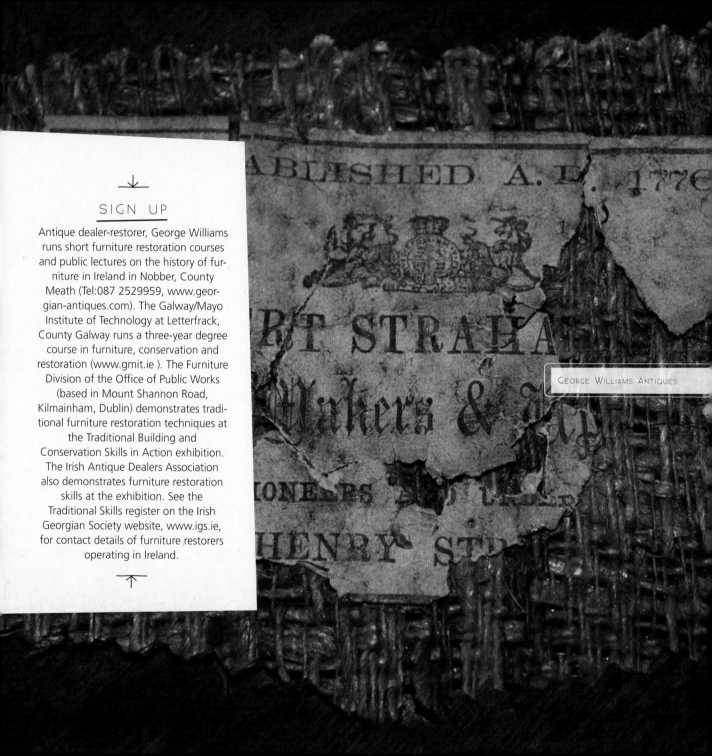

SIGN UP

Antique dealer-restorer, George Williams runs short furniture restoration courses and public lectures on the history of furniture in Ireland in Nobber, County Meath (Tel:087 2529959, www.georgian-antiques.com). The Galway/Mayo Institute of Technology at Letterfrack, County Galway runs a three-year degree course in furniture, conservation and restoration (www.gmit.ie). The Furniture Division of the Office of Public Works (based in Mount Shannon Road, Kilmainham, Dublin) demonstrates traditional furniture restoration techniques at the Traditional Building and Conservation Skills in Action exhibition. The Irish Antique Dealers Association also demonstrates furniture restoration skills at the exhibition. See the Traditional Skills register on the Irish Georgian Society website, www.igs.ie, for contact details of furniture restorers operating in Ireland.

GEORGE WILLIAMS ANTIQUES

THE REPAIR OF LIME POINTING

What is it?

Lime pointing describes the process by which the joints between bricks or stone are filled in with a narrow ridge of lime putty, or a mortar mix of lime and sand. Pointing is the material that holds the bricks together and is generally used on the outside of a building. Traditional forms of pointing can also be used to improve the appearance of poor brickwork.

Lime has been used for thousands of years in construction. In fact, old maps of Ireland show limekilns in almost every roadside field in rural areas. Traditional construction in Ireland involved the use of stone and brick bedded down in lime mortar. As far back as the eleventh century and indeed earlier, tower houses, abbeys and castles were all built from stone and brick with the use of lime mortar for building. Throughout the following centuries, the basic building materials remained the same and buildings were plastered (rendered) and painted. In the nineteenth century, more important buildings were dressed with stone or brick and the joints were pointed using lime.

Lime was gradually replaced by cement in the twentieth century because cement was deemed to be cheap, easier to use and it dried more quickly. Industrialisation brought mass production of cement throughout Ireland and traditional construction with lime was deemed to be old-fashioned. As a result, many of the traditional lime techniques began to die out and older buildings were inexpertly pointed with cement. This often led to cracking and unnecessary damage to the brickwork and stone.

The problem with using cement rather than lime in older buildings was precisely because it hardens so well. By hardening so fast and so strongly, cement doesn't allow any movement of the brickwork, which would prevent cracking of bricks over time. Neither is it porous so it doesn't allow the building materials to breathe, which would prevent a build up of dampness. If maintained in their original state, older buildings – with their thick walls and lime mortars and pointing – should be dry and warm but if cement is used, they are cold and water is trapped internally. Indeed, according to conservation architect Gráinne Shaffrey, 'if joints are re-pointed using dense cement, the rain falls on the brickwork and is absorbed into the brick rather than evaporating out through the lime joint. The edges of brick begin to weather and decay while the cement joint remains intact. You get the reverse of what you want.'

An interest in the use of lime for pointing and other aspects of building work, including the rendering of external walls, has re-developed in the last twenty-five years or so. People began to realise that it is much better for restoration work on old buildings. Knowledge of traditional pointing techniques is increasing all the time and some brick repair masons are now re-using the wigging techniques that were traditional to Dublin in the nineteenth century.

How is it done?

There are several different types of pointing. These include tuck-pointing, wigging pointing and simple flush pointing. With flush pointing, the joint and pointing are on the same level as the brickwork. This weatherproofs the building, as well as being aesthetically pleasing. More advanced forms of pointing are used to cover over poor brickwork, dating back to the Georgian era.

What do the experts say?

Derek Bacon is a fourth generation lime pointer who still uses traditional techniques to repair lime pointing. 'First, we take out the old mortar and then repair the bricks where necessary, before re-pointing with new lime mortar,' he explains. 'The tools haven't changed much over the years. We use trowels and a hawk for the pointing but we also sometimes use more modern tools to extract the old mortar or for preparing materials.'

How long does it take?

That depends on the size of the area to be worked on and the type of pointing used. More elaborate styles take longer to do. Recently, Derek Bacon worked on a double-fronted Georgian house on Henrietta Street in Dublin and it took almost a year to repair and re-point the whole building, using the tuck-pointing technique. You can see examples of his work at www.baconrestorations.ie.

Where can I see good examples of lime-pointing used in buildings?

Pat McAfee's book, *Limeworks*, has many close-up photographs of lime used in modern and traditional buildings. See www.buildinglimesforumireland.com for more details.

↓

SIGN UP

The repair of lime pointing is a technical skill that requires training and practice. The Irish Georgian Society runs occasional lecture series in conserving period houses. These evening lectures often include a talk on the use of lime by conservation architects, Grainne Shaffrey and Susan Roundtree. See www.igs.ie for details. The Building Limes Forum Ireland actively promotes the use of lime mortar through workshops and demonstrations. The Dublin Civic Trust also run occasional masterclasses on the conservation and repair of render and masonry (Tel:01 4756911, www.dublincivictrust.ie).

Limeworks: Using Lime in Traditional and New Buildings by Patrick McAfee (Building Limes Forum Ireland) is an excellent guide to the many uses of lime for construction and restoration.

↑

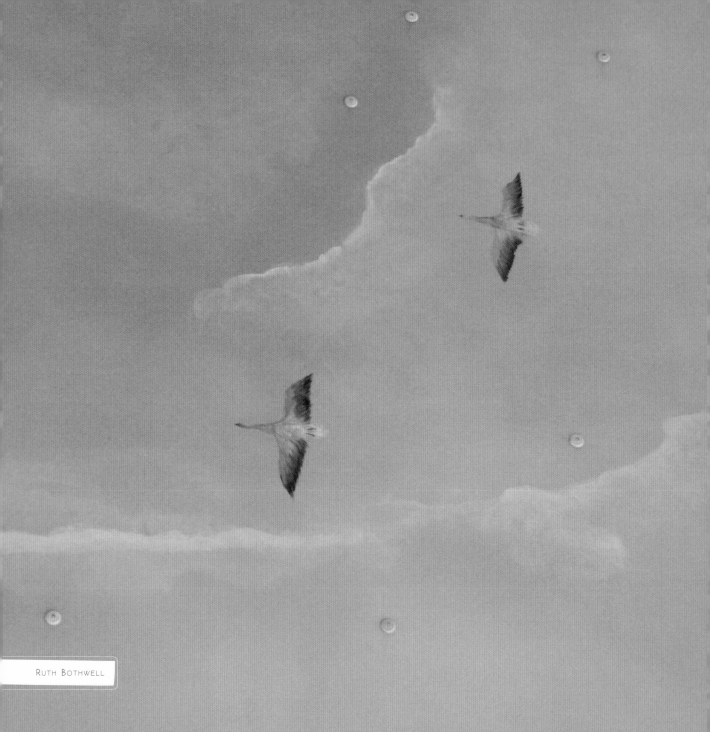

RUTH BOTHWELL

DECORATIVE PAINTING AND CONSERVATION

What is it?

Decorative painting is the application of paint to a surface to create form, colour and detail. Decorative art began when primitive people adorned their caves with hunting scenes. Many symbols and patterns which have become standard decorative motifs are derived from early Greek, Roman and Egyptian decoration. Decorative painting includes ceiling paintings, wall painting and murals, painted and stenciled patterns, marbling, wood graining, gilding, trompe l'oeil and fresco painting. Any surface can be painted – ceilings, walls, capitols, columns, doors, joinery, furniture, objects, fittings and floors – if prepared in the appropriate manner.

As with all decorative features, decorative painting changed in style from its prehistoric roots, through the splendor of the Renaissance and Baroque periods, to more subtle Neo-Classical and Romantic periods. Architecture and art were at their most ornate and dramatic during the Baroque and Rococo periods. One of the great achievements of this era were the amazing ceiling paintings by Giambattista Tiepolo, the finest decorative painter of eighteenth-century Europe.

Some ornate plasterwork ceilings of eighteenth-century Dublin houses incorporated individual painted panels, or roundels, as part of the overall decorative scheme. In his book *Decorative Dublin*, Peter Pearson says that in rare cases, some houses had the entire wall surfaces of one or even two rooms decorated with murals. An idealised classical landscape was the favourite subject of such decorative paintings.

The Neo-Classical period brought a new lightness with pastel colours used in a more gentle form of decoration. The Romanticism of the nineteenth century in Europe brought a new freedom in decoration with influences from Moorish, Gothic, Byzantine, Renaissance, Celtic and folk art.

Throughout the Arts and Crafts movement, decorative painting flourished triumphantly. Craftsmen from great European cities such as Paris and London were using marbling and wood graining to great effect in churches, public buildings, shops and private homes. Harry Clarke and his brother, Walter pioneered decorative arts in Ireland in the 1920s and 1930s. As well as their famous stained glass windows, their studio produced painted and decorative panels for churches.

Over the years, murals, stencils and wall paintings were covered over by panels, paint or paper, only to be rediscovered years later. Nowadays, there is a greater appreciation of the time and skill required to carry out this decorative work. And, the approach to their conservation and preservation recognises and values the traditional approaches used.

How is it done?

Decorative treatments must be carefully planned and researched to ensure the correct method is used for the space and surface. It is usually carried out in situ but smaller murals and wall panels can be prepared and painted onto canvas or board in a studio. Murals are painted in oil, acrylic, gouache, tempera or watercolour. An oil glaze, combined with artists' oils, was traditionally used for marbling, wood graining and broken colour. However nowadays, an acrylic glaze is preferred for health and environmental reasons. Gilding is the application of gold, silver or metal leaf onto a surface and is generally used to emphasise detail on mirrors, frames, icons or exterior features such as weather vanes, finials and facades.

What about conservation?

Conservation of a decorative area requires research and detailed preliminary inspection of the fabric and history of the building. This is to understand the materials and construction methods of the original surface and subsequent repairs. This information determines the methods and techniques used to restore damaged areas. Paint analysis is sometimes used for historical accuracy and to ensure the correct conservation approach is used. This information is recorded for use by future conservators.

What do the experts say?

'It is best to save as much of the existing decoration as possible and to record,

RUTH BOTHWE

RUTH BOTHWELL

consolidate, stabilise and retouch where necessary, using natural reversible products,' says Ruth Bothwell, a paintings conservator and decorative artist based in Belfast (www.decowellrestoration.com).

How long does it take?

The length of a conservation project depends on the extent of damage to the surfaces, the accessibility to the area, the time and money allocated for the restoration and the qualified personnel available to do the job. For example, work on a large ceiling or historical painting can take months, if not years to complete, whereas spot repairs on a wood-grained door can take only a couple of hours.

Where can I see examples of good decorative paint effects?

The richly colourful interior of University Church, St Stephen's Green, Dublin has fine decorative painting by English artist John Hungerford Pollen. St Eunan's Cathedral in Letterkenny has some fine examples of decorated ceiling panels, which have been recently restored by Decowell. St Mary's Church on Haddington Road, Dublin shows an example of recently gilded ceiling details.

The dramatic eighteenth-century painted ceiling by Italian artist Vincenzo Valdré in St Patrick's Hall, Dublin Castle can be seen on guided tours (Tel:01 6458813, www.dublincastle.ie). Other examples of fine decorative painting can be seen in the Royal Irish Academy of Music, Westland Row, Dublin, as well as the Dublin Writers Museum, Parnell Square, Dublin. Rathfarnham Castle in Rathfarnham, Dublin also has fine examples of panels painted by the eighteenth-century artist Angelica Kaufmann.

SIGN UP

Decorative painting and conservation is a very specialised skill. International training colleges who focus on the craft include the Institute Superieur de Peinture, Van Der Kelen School of Decorative Arts in Brussels, Belgium; The London School of Picture and Frame Restoration and the Caurtauld Institute of Art in London. Ruth Bothwell from Decowell holds demonstrations on decorative art at the annual Traditional Building and Conservation Skills in Action exhibition. Contact details for decorative artists can be found on the Irish Georgian Society traditional building and conservation skills register of practitioners (www.igs.ie), and on the Irish Crafts Council of Ireland website (www.ccoi.ie).

DIRECTORY OF CRAFT GUILDS, ASSOCIATIONS, NETWORKS AND SOCIETIES

Ceramics Ireland

Ceramics Ireland was established in 1977 and is made up of artists, craftspeople, collectors and friends of the society who are primarily based throughout Ireland. It aims to foster creativity, passion and excellence, raising the standard, quality and profile of all ceramic activity in Ireland. For further details, visit www.ceramicsireland.org.

Contemporary Tapestry Artists Ireland

Contemporary Tapestry Artists Ireland is comprised of professional tapestry weavers who design and make original works primarily in the Gobelin tapestry technique. The aim of the group is to promote woven tapestry in Ireland, creating a greater awareness of this medium and an appreciation of its richness and variety of execution.

DLR Jewellery Designers

DLR Jewellery Designers Network is organised and facilitated by Dun Laoghaire Rathdown County Enterprise Board. The objective of the Network is to raise the profile of jewellery companies within the Dun Laoghaire Rathdown area, support internationalisation and enhance marketing and collaboration. For further details, visit www.dlrjewellerydesigners.ie.

Estate Yard Printmakers

Estate Yard Printmakers is a group of artists and makers, which was formed in December 2009 to establish an open access print studio in Kilkenny. The group aims to promote print as an artform, to encourage the use of non-toxic methods and to improve the standard of printmaking by providing facilities and training.

Feltmakers Ireland

Feltmakers Ireland is a national organisation that provides workshops, exhibitions and information about feltmaking, not only for members but for anyone interested in feltwork. Four workshops are held annually and are open to anyone to attend. Feltmakers Ireland is a member of the International Feltmakers Association. For further details, visit www.feltmakersireland.com.

Federation of Jewellery Manufacturers of Ireland (FJMI)

The Federation of Jewellery Manufacturers of Ireland was established in 1963 to coordinate the manufacture of jewellery in Ireland. FJMI members undertake to abide by a strict code of ethics, giving assurance to customers that jewellery items purchased from members have been crafted with care, skill and pride. For further details, visit www.fjmi.com.

Filament Fibre Artists

Filament is a network of fibre artists living and working in Ireland and aims to provide mutual support and to promote fibre arts. Filament artists work together to pursue excellence in fibre art and develop public awareness of this dynamic discipline. For further details, visit www.filamentfibreartists.wordpress.com.

Glass Society of Ireland

The Glass Society of Ireland is an informal network set up to share information on events, exhibitions and opportunities among glassmakers, collectors, historians and enthusiasts. Its aim is to communicate the value of glass among members and to a wider audience. For further details, visit www.glasssocietyofireland.blogspot.com.

Guild of Irish Lacemakers

The Guild of Irish Lacemakers was founded in 1987 to assist all lacemakers, especially those making traditional Irish Laces. The objective of the Guild is to further develop lace and lace design in Ireland through workshops, lectures, exhibitions and other activities of interest to lacemakers.

Handweavers Guild of Cork

The Handweavers Guild of Cork was established in the 1980s as a practising group of weavers, spinners, dyers and felters. The aim of the Guild is to promote these crafts and to improve the standard of work by running regular workshops and exchanging information at their monthly meetings.

Irish Artist Blacksmiths Association (IABA)

The Irish Artists Blacksmiths Association was set up to encourage, advise and promote artists, blacksmiths and decorative metal workers working in Ireland. IABA members offer both classical and contemporary decorative metal work from large architectural commissions to small domestic items forged and made with skilled hands. For further details, visit www.irishblacksmiths.com.

Irish Basketmakers Association

The Irish Basketmakers Association aims to improve the standard of basketmaking and increase awareness of this ancient craft, as well as encouraging contact and co-operation between basketmakers. The Association seeks to achieve this by promoting courses and masterclasses, giving demonstrations at shows and including work in exhibitions. For further details, visit www.irishbasketmakers.ie.

Irish Chairmakers

The Irish Chairmakers group was set up with the aim of developing a higher profile for chairmakers in Ireland whose work is of a high standard, and to help increase the viability of small chair-making businesses. The group also works towards organising annual chair exhibitions.

Irish Guild of Embroiderers

The Irish Guild of Embroiderers was set up for the benefit of everyone interested in learning more about needlework, both traditional and innovative, experimenting with unusual techniques and materials and exhibiting new work. The Guild membership is made up of professional practitioners, hobbyist and enthusiasts. For further details, visit www.irishguildofembroiderers.com.

Irish Guild of Weavers, Spinners & Dyers

The Irish Guild of Weavers, Spinners & Dyers is a voluntary organisation formed to preserve, improve and promote expertise in hand-weaving, spinning and dying and to encourage excellence in craftsmanship, texture, colour and design. Workshops, lectures, exhibitions and demonstrations are organised throughout the year. For further details, visit www.weavers.ie.

Irish Paper Artists Associations

The Irish Paper Artists Association was established in 2010 to raise awareness and appreciation for the ancient art and craft of hand paper. The group encourages networking exchange internationally, by connecting with similar guilds and groups abroad and by linking with IAPMA (International Association of hand Papermaking and paper Artists).

Irish Patchwork Society

The Irish Patchwork Society was founded in 1981 to promote the practice and art of patchwork, appliqué and quilting in Ireland. The Society promotes lectures, workshops, exhibitions and other activities of interest to quiltmakers, while aiming to maintain or raise the standard of quiltmaking in Ireland. For further details, visit www.irishpatchwork.ie.

Irish Woodturners' Guild

The aim of the Irish Woodturners' Guild is to offer mutual help and encouragement to woodturners of all levels. The objective of the Guild is to exchange information, assist in improving design and technical skills, to promote woodturning to the general public, organise seminars and exhibitions and to publish regular journals. For further details, visit www.irishwoodturnersguild.com.

Lettercarvers Guild Ireland

The Lettercarvers Guild of Ireland was founded to promote quality hand-carved lettering in stone by trained craftspeople. A further aim of the Guild is the guardianship of the heritage of lettering in Ireland and to advance the awareness and protection of this historical legacy in stone. For further details, visit www.lettercarversguild.ie.

Na Píobairí Uilleann

The Society of Uilleann Pipers, known as Na Píobairí Uilleann, was founded in 1968 with the aim of perpetuating the spirit of Irish music, particularly in the playing of the pipes, the production and maintenance of the instrument itself. and the teaching of the Uilleann pipes, especially to young people. For further details, visit www.pipers.ie.

Peannairí

Peannairí (Irish Scribes) is a society of calligraphers based in Dublin with an aim to encourage and nurture the calligrapher's craft and the development of fine writing in Ireland. Regular classes and workshops on different aspects of calligraphy or related crafts are taught by experienced calligraphers. For further details, visit www.calligraphy.ie.

Print Block

Print Block is a Dublin-based artist collective and non-profit organisation, which provides professional artists, craftspeople and designers with shared working surfaces and equipment for the production of printed textiles. It aims to provide and promote a supportive workshop environment for the making of textile art, design. For further details, visit www.printblock.tumblr.com

The Quilters Guild of Ireland

The Quilters' Guild of Ireland provides education about patchwork, appliqué and quilting to members in Northern Ireland and the Republic of Ireland as well as internationally. The guild offers education to all members through workshops and clinics taught by recognised teachers. For further details, visit www.theqgi.com.

Society of Cork Potters

The Society of Cork Potters was formally founded in 1980 by a group of potters and ceramic artists working in County Cork. The aim of the Society is to run Cork-based, Ceramic-specific networking events, workshops and exhibitions for the benefit of its members. For further details, visit www.societyofcorkpotters.wordpress.com.

Many discipline specific craft groups have been established throughout Ireland. For more information on craft guilds, associations, networks and societies, visit the Crafts Council of Ireland website at www.ccoi.ie.

BIBLIOGRAPHY

Ball, Michael. *Decorative Glasswork*. Photography by Peter Williams. London: Lorenz Books, 1998.

Ellis, Sian, Paul Felix and Tom Quinn. *The Book of Forgotten Crafts: Keeping the Traditions Alive*. Devon: David & Charles Publishers, 2011.

Finch, Janet. *The Art and Craft of Jewellery*. Photography by Kevin Summers. London: Mitchell Beazley, 1992.

Hickie, David ed. *Irish Hedgerows: Networks for Nature*. Dublin: Environmental Publications Ltd, 2004.

Hogan, Joe. *Basketmaking in Ireland*. In association with The Heritage Council. Dublin: Wordwell, 2001.

McAfee, Patrick. *Irish Stone Walls*. Dublin: O'Brien Press, 1997.

McAfee, Patrick. *Limeworks: Using Lime in Traditional and New Buildings*. Dublin: The Building Limes Forum Ireland, 2009.

Ospina, Alison. *Green Wood Chairs – Chairs and Chairmakers of Ireland*. Stobart Davies: UK, 2009.

Pearson, Peter. *Decorative Dublin*. Dublin: O'Brien Press, 2002.

Peterson, Jan and Susan Peterson. *Working with Clay*. 3rd edition. London: Laurence King Publishing, 2009.

Seymour, John. *The Forgotten Arts & Crafts*. UK: DK Publishing, 2001.

Shaw-Smith, David, dir. *HANDS: Documentaries on Irish Traditional Crafts*. Produced for RTÉ Television in conjunction with the Film Corporation of Ireland.

Shaw-Smith, David. *Traditional Crafts of Ireland*. London: Thames & Hudson, 2003.

Stribley, Miriam. *The Calligraphy Source Book*. London; Little, Brown, 1993.

Warnes, Jon. *Living Willow Sculpture*. Kent: Search Press, 2000.

PHOTOGRAPH CREDITS

⊚ Crafts Council of Ireland

The Crafts Council of Ireland (CCoI) is the main champion of the craft industry in Ireland, fostering its growth and commercial strength, communicating its unique identity and stimulating quality design, innovation and competitiveness. Headquartered in Kilkenny, CCoI has over 2,600 registered clients on its register of craft enterprises and has over 70 member organisations. As well as being designed Year of Craft, 2011 also marked CCoI's 40th anniversary. The organisation's activities are funded by the Department of Jobs, Enterprise and Innovation via Enterprise Ireland.

For further information, please visit www.ccoi.ie.

An Chomhairle Oidhreachta
The Heritage Council

The Heritage Council's vision is that the value of Ireland's heritage is enjoyed, managed and protected for the vital contribution it makes to our identity, well-being and future.

The Heritage Council is a public body working in the public interest. Our priorities are to support jobs, education and heritage tourism in local communities. The Heritage Council is energetic, flexible and innovative in supporting communities to care for the national heritage. By putting in place infrastructure and networks to enable communities to take responsibility for and participate in the development and conservation of their heritage assets, a difference is being made and jobs are being created. Success is measurable and readily identifiable.

For further information visit www.heritagecouncil.ie.